PRAISE FOR THE CHRI~

I am excited to see these biblically grounded and theologically astute materials, birthed out of a mission to create resources for the global church, have a greater reach through their publication in print!
> —**Andrew Abernethy**, Associate Professor of Old Testament, Wheaton College, Wheaton College Graduate School

The Christian Essentials series provides a wonderful service to the church of the Lord Jesus Christ. It is theologically rich without being dense. Scholars, pastors, and laypersons will find these works immensely valuable.
> —**Daniel Akin**, President, Southeastern Baptist Theological Seminary

There is no doubt that Richard Pratt and Third Millennium Ministries are providing an extraordinarily useful and fruitful service of theological education to Christians around the world. I have seen the abundant fruit of their labors and am profoundly grateful for their work.
> —**Bruce P. Baugus**, Associate Professor of Philosophy and Theology, Reformed Theological Seminary, Jackson

This exciting new series brings the basic truths of our Christian faith to a wide public audience at a time when doing so is more needed than ever. Church study groups in particular will benefit from this important resource, which should be widely used in Christian education programs everywhere.
> —**Gerald Bray**, Research Professor of Divinity, Beeson Divinity School

Third Millennium Ministries has done an outstanding job of making an orthodox theological education available to many who would otherwise lack access. I am delighted that a crucial part of this material is now appearing in printed form.
> —**Gareth Lee Cockerill**, Professor Emeritus of New Testament and Biblical Theology, Wesley Biblical Seminary

Third Millennium's theological resources explain complex theology in terms anyone can understand. I am happy to see these volumes appear in print for the first time. They are suitable for pastors, students, and laypeople—anyone who seeks to understand the coherent teaching of the Bible and why it matters today.

— **Brandon Crowe**, Professor of New Testament, Westminster
  Theological Seminary

Third Millennium's books stand in the great tradition of orthodox Christianity. They are grounded in Scripture, they rest on the work of godly experts, and they will prove beneficial for church leaders and disciples alike. These works will serve God's people worldwide for many years.

— **Dan Doriani**, Professor of Biblical and Systematic Theology,
  Covenant Theological Seminary

This series represents the culmination of years of research, teaching, and outreach. Hammered out on the anvil of experience, it is highly accessible while being doctrinally solid. It should be acquired and used by every serious Christian, whatever their language, whatever their challenges, whatever their stage of maturity.

— **William Edgar**, Professor of Apologetics, Westminster Theological
  Seminary

I have been using Third Millennium's materials for over ten years, both personally and professionally. The academic and theologically sound instructions, along with practical applications, allow people to become equipped for ministry without leaving their homes or home countries.

— **Thad James Jr.**, Vice President, Birmingham Theological Seminary

For over two decades, Third Millennium Ministries has provided to church leaders around the world, in many languages, through various media, and without charge, robust theological education that is clear and biblical, expressing the consensus of Reformational Christians. I believe that this series will do much to equip readers with a sound grasp of the great truths of God's Word.

— **Dennis E. Johnson**, Professor Emeritus of Practical Theology,
  Westminster Seminary California

The Christian Essentials series presents theology in the way theology ought to be presented—fresh, balanced, accessible, and engaging. Written under the authority of Scripture with a keen eye to the needs of the church, the texts systematically unpack the great doctrines of our faith in ways that are practical and pastoral. I'm glad to recommend the series.

—**Ken D. Keathley**, Jesse Hendley Endowed Chair of Biblical Theology, Southeastern Baptist Theological Seminary

In this series of short books, the biblical and historical evidence for belief in the triune God is presented in clear and easily accessible form. An excellent survey of these doctrines written in a worshipful and practical style, they will help the reader not only to know about God but to know him intimately and to serve him faithfully.

—**Glenn R. Kreider**, Acting Chair and Professor of Theological Studies, Dallas Theological Seminary

Third Millennium Ministries has created an orthodox, international, accessible, and wonderfully produced set of video resources on the essentials of the Christian faith. Now their excellent resources are becoming available in print for readers worldwide. This is indeed a blessing for God's people—these are ideal resources for discipleship and study groups.

—**Fredrick J. Long**, Professor of New Testament, Asbury Theological Seminary

These books provide excellent material not only for the individual believer but for group studies in churches that are committed to maintaining a firm grasp of the faith once delivered to the saints.

—**Thomas J. Nettles**, Visiting Professor of Historical Theology, Southwestern Baptist Theological Seminary

Third Millennium Ministries is strategically putting top-notch theological training materials into the hands of Christian leaders around the world. I'm pleased to commend these books for the building up of the body of Christ.

—**Robert L. Plummer**, Collin and Evelyn Aikman Professor of Biblical Studies, The Southern Baptist Theological Seminary

Third Millennium Ministries has pulled together an exceptional team of pastors, theologians, and Bible scholars to write a biblically sound, theologically informed, practically oriented curriculum for personal study and for use in schools and churches. Now available in book form for the first time, this series will help bi-vocational pastors, Bible study leaders, youth directors, college and high school students, and many others to further their theological education in the tradition of the Reformation.
   —**Philip Ryken**, President, Wheaton College

The books in the Christian Essentials series provide a thoughtful, accessible articulation of the main tenets of classic Christian belief. By drawing together insights and perspectives from a breadth of orthodox Christian theologians, these books confirm that the basic contours of the always relevant faith once delivered to the saints are wonderfully consistent and shared.
   —**Glen G. Scorgie**, Professor of Theology, Bethel Seminary San Diego

The welcome addition of print books to Third Millennium's repertoire will expand their reach and impact. This is good news for the Good News!
   —**Mark L. Strauss**, University Professor of New Testament, Bethel
      Seminary San Diego

Third Millennium is an outstanding ministry that provides top-notch theological resources for the church around the world. I pray that God will use these books on doctrine to strengthen the people of God around the world, for his glory, and for the advance of the gospel.
   —**Erik Thoennes**, Professor of Theology, Talbot School of Theology,
      Biola University

The curriculum of Third Millennium Ministries is robustly biblical and joyfully evangelical. I'm glad that such resources expand global access to clear teaching from God's Word. Readers will encounter a focused and gracious set of Protestant perspectives from reputable and pastoral scholars.
   —**Daniel J. Treier**, Knoedler Professor of Theology, Wheaton College,
      Wheaton College Graduate School

THE ATTRIBUTES
AND WORK OF GOD

CHRISTIAN ESSENTIALS

The Attributes and Work of God
The Life and Work of Jesus
The Nature and Work of the Holy Spirit

THE ATTRIBUTES AND WORK OF GOD

CHRISTIAN ESSENTIALS

RICHARD L. PRATT JR.

SERIES EDITORS

Richard L. Pratt Jr., General Editor
Ra McLaughlin, General Editor
Cindy Sawyer, Associate General Editor
Scott Simmons, Assistant Editor
Lauren Denney, Assistant Editor

P&R PUBLISHING
P.O. BOX 817 • PHILLIPSBURG • NEW JERSEY 08865-0817

This book has been adapted from the video series *We Believe in God*. Copyright © 2015 by Third Millennium Ministries, Inc. All rights reserved. Interviews in sidebars have been edited for this format.

Unless otherwise indicated, all Scripture quotations are from the HOLY BIBLE, NEW INTERNATIONAL VERSION®. NIV®. Copyright © 1973, 1978, 1984 by International Bible Society. Used by permission of Zondervan Publishing House. All rights reserved.

Scripture quotations marked ESV are from The Holy Bible, English Standard Version® (ESV®). Copyright © 2001 by Crossway Bibles, a division of Good News Publishers. Used by permission. All rights reserved.

Scripture quotations marked NASB are taken from the New American Standard Bible®, Copyright © 1960, 1962, 1963, 1968, 1971, 1972, 1973, 1975, 1977, 1995 by The Lockman Foundation. Used by permission.

Scripture quotations marked NRSV are taken from the *New Revised Standard Version of the Bible*, Copyright © 1989, by the Division of Christian Education of the National Council of the Churches of Christ in the United States of America. Used by permission. All rights reserved.

Italics within Scripture quotations indicates emphasis added.

Quotations from the Augsburg Confession are taken from *The Augsburg Confession*, trans. Gerhard F. Bente and W. H. T. Dau (St. Louis: Concordia, 1921).

Quotations from the Belgic Confession are taken from Philip Schaff, ed., *The Creeds of Christendom, with a History and Critical Notes*, vol. 3, *The Evangelical Protestant Creeds*, 4th ed. (repr., Grand Rapids: Baker Book House, 1969).

Printed in the United States of America

Library of Congress Cataloging-in-Publication Data

Names: Pratt, Richard L., 1953- author.
Title: The attributes and work of God / Richard L. Pratt, Jr.
Description: Phillipsburg, New Jersey : P&R Publishing, [2022] | Series: Christian essentials | Includes bibliographical references and index. | Summary: "We can't understand ourselves or our world without knowing God. Designed for formal or informal study, this book explores God's plan, works, and attributes and answers key questions about him"-- Provided by publisher.
Identifiers: LCCN 2021021667 | ISBN 9781629954707 (paperback) | ISBN 9781629954714 (epub)
Subjects: LCSH: God (Christianity)--Textbooks. | God (Christianity)--Attributes--Textbooks.
Classification: LCC BT108 .P73 2021 | DDC 231--dc23
LC record available at https://lccn.loc.gov/2021021667

CONTENTS

ABOUT THE CHRISTIAN ESSENTIALS SERIES

The volumes in this series have been adapted from a video seminary curriculum produced by Third Millennium Ministries. Because Third Millennium writes and produces this curriculum for a global, multilingual, evangelical audience, some aspects of this series may surprise readers. For example, we don't always follow Western pedagogical and andragogical traditions. We often organize and address subjects differently from more traditional texts. We also tend to prefer language that is easily translatable into languages that don't yet have robust theological vocabularies. As a result, we use fewer academic and theological terms than do traditional works on the same subjects.

Finally, while we don't promote ideas that contradict our doctrinal standards (the Westminster Confession of Faith, together with its Larger and Shorter Catechisms), we value and include the thoughts, insights, and wisdom the Holy Spirit has provided to those outside the Reformed tradition. We sincerely believe that Bible-believing Christians of every evangelical tradition are united by far, far more than they are divided by. For this reason, the interviews found in the sidebars throughout these volumes often come from professors and pastors in traditions different from our own. We hope that readers will find in these interviews opportunities for valuing, admiring, and learning from our brothers and sisters in different traditions.

For more information on our video curriculum, please visit thirdmill.org.

Ra McLaughlin
General Editor

ACKNOWLEDGMENTS

This volume would not have been possible without the entire team at Third Millennium Ministries that produced the video series from which this present book was adapted. Special thanks go to our script editorial team (Scott Simmons, Mitchell Cooper, Cindy Sawyer, Jann Eckenwiler, and Kristy Spanjer), our graphics team (Eric Linares, Careth Turner, Ben Baxter, David Schuster, Sean Luo, David Zoeller, and Stephanie Mathis), our videography team (Jim Southard, Scott Simmons, and Mitchell Cooper), and our sound team (Chris Russell, Peter Sorrel, and Jeremy Birdsall).

Very special thanks go to the seminaries and churches that graciously provided interviewees and interview locations for the videos: African Christian University, Zambia; Apologetics Resource Center; Biblical Theological Seminary; Birmingham Theological Seminary; Briarwood Presbyterian Church, Birmingham; Christ Community Church, Laguna Hills; College Church, Wheaton, Illinois; Concordia Seminary; Dallas Theological Seminary; East Asia School of Theology; Gordon-Conwell Theological Seminary; Grace and Peace Fellowship, St. Louis; Knox Theological Seminary; North India Institute of Theological Studies; North Park Church, Wexford, Pennsylvania; Reformed Theological Seminary; Roosevelt Community Church, Phoenix; Second Presbyterian Church, Greenville; Second

Presbyterian Church, Memphis, Tennessee; Stephen Tong Evangelistic Ministries International; Talbot School of Theology; The Austin Stone Community Church; Trinity Downtown, Orlando; Trinity Evangelical Divinity School; Trinity School for Ministry; Wesley Biblical Seminary; Westminster Theological Seminary; Wheaton College; and Wheaton College Graduate School.

INTRODUCTION:
A NOTE TO THE READER

"Do you believe in God?" The answers are usually straightforward. Some answer yes. Others say no. Still others reply, "I'm not sure." But if we follow up by asking, "What do you believe *about* God?" we get all kinds of answers, even from faithful followers of Christ.

The Bible has so much to say about God that faithful Christians have followed many legitimate directions as they have summarized its teachings. This volume highlights the mainstream of evangelical systematic theology. For our purposes, the term *evangelical* means theology that acknowledges the full authority of Scripture. *Systematic theology* refers to longstanding, traditional ways of expressing the underlying logical system of biblical teachings.

The Bible itself expresses its teachings about God in narratives, laws, songs, prophecies, proverbs, and letters—to name just a few. So, if you are not familiar with the emphases of traditional systematic theology, you may be surprised by some of the things you read in this volume. They will not be entirely unfamiliar. These chapters reflect vocabulary and categories familiar to leaders in many branches of the church, but new students of theology may encounter unfamiliar terrain.

Think of this book as an opportunity to learn what the Holy Spirit has taught the body of Christ to emphasize over the centuries. It's a chance to gain wisdom in preparation for your own exploration of the Scriptures. A careful study of the doctrine of God, or "theology proper" as it has been called, will enable you to be "a worker who has no need to be ashamed, rightly handling the word of truth" (2 Tim. 2:15 ESV).

Richard L. Pratt Jr.

PART 1

WHAT WE KNOW ABOUT GOD

Knowing God means different things to different people—everything from experiencing personal intimacy with God, to witnessing his mighty works, to understanding facts about him that the Holy Spirit has revealed. Most followers of Christ realize that it's valuable to have a personal relationship with God and to see him at work in the world, but unfortunately, many of us don't sense that it's equally important to learn as many facts about God as we can. It's no wonder. Studying what traditional systematic theologians often call "the doctrine of God," or "theology proper," is so complex that it requires a great deal of effort. However, as difficult as it may be, the more we learn about God, the more our personal relationship with him grows, and the more our awareness of his work in the world grows. In fact, understanding as much as we can about God strengthens every dimension of our Christian faith.

DIVINE REVELATION

It would be difficult to imagine a more fundamental issue as we study the doctrine of God than divine revelation. What has God disclosed about himself? How has he done this? Our answers to these questions set the course for every facet of theology proper.

For our purposes, we can summarize the basic Christian idea of divine revelation in this way: divine revelation is God's self-disclosure, always given in human terms and most fully given in Christ.

DIVINE REVELATION IS ALWAYS GIVEN IN HUMAN TERMS

We all know that we can't study God like we do so many other things in daily life. We can't measure his height and weight or put him in a test tube and examine him. On the contrary, God is transcendent, so far beyond us that he would be entirely hidden except for one fact: the Holy Spirit has revealed truths about God to us in human terms. Systematic theologians have often spoken of this as the "anthropomorphic" character of revelation. In other words, God has disclosed himself in human form, or in ways that human beings can understand. There are at least four kinds of anthropomorphic revelation in the Scriptures.

One of the most amazing things about the God of the Bible is *unique* to the God of the Bible: He maintains all his incommunicable attributes—infinite attributes such as sovereignty and eternality and infinity—even as he relates to creatures in history who are time-bound and finite. Not only that, the great I AM enters into time, space, and human history in relationship with creatures and relates to them on their level.

This doesn't mean he sacrifices any of his all-knowing, infinite, eternal nature, but he relates to his creatures right on the level where they are, much as we would do for a little child, and speaks to them on that level. If I walk into our kitchen and see flour all over the place and say, "Honey, did something happen with the flour?" it's not because I don't know something happened with the flour. Rather, I'm relating to my children right where they are. And that's what God does for us in his grace.

This is an amazing condescension of God—so much so that at times it seems as though he must be compromising some of his eternal, infinite characteristics, but that's never the case. God is simply relating to us on our level because he loves us that much. **K. Erik Thoennes**

Human Characteristics

In the narrowest sense, the Scriptures often compare God's characteristics to human characteristics. Numerous biblical passages speak of God as having eyes, ears, nostrils, arms, hands, legs, and feet. The Scriptures as a whole make it clear that these kinds of anthropomorphisms are to be taken as metaphors—comparisons between God and human beings. God doesn't have physical eyes or hands like people do, but we know, nonetheless, that he sees and accomplishes things all the time. God also reasons, asks questions, consults others, feels emotions, and ponders. He takes action and relents, much like human beings do.

Social Structures

In a slightly broader sense, the Scriptures also present God anthropomorphically in terms of human social structures. For instance, the Bible frequently depicts God as the supreme King of creation. He sits on his throne in heaven, holds counsel, hears reports, makes announcements, sends messengers, and receives worship, similar to the ways human emperors did in biblical times. Along these same lines, Scripture portrays God as Israel's royal warrior, the lawgiver, the covenant maker, and the covenant keeper. He's the royal shepherd and the royal husband and father of his people. Once again, these revelations of God tell us that God is like human beings in certain ways. He rules in ways that are similar to the ways human kings ruled in the ancient world.

Visible Appearances

Even more broadly, we can say that God's visible appearances in history are also anthropomorphic. The Bible reports a number of times when God appeared visibly in the world—what we often call "theophanies." The most dramatic theophanies associated God with physical smoke and fire and with visions of his visible heavenly cloud of glory. Now, passages like Colossians 1:15 and 1 Timothy 1:17 tell us that God himself is invisible. So these visible appearances of God are also anthropomorphic in the sense that they don't present God as he knows himself. Rather, they present God in ways that we human beings can experience him with our limited capacities.

Abstract Qualities

Finally, in the broadest sense, the Scriptures also reveal God in human terms even when they refer to his abstract qualities. The Bible often speaks of God as being just, holy, powerful, and the like, but biblical authors explained these abstract descriptions of God in human terms, in ways that we can understand. So it's fair to say that, in one way or another, all divine revelation is anthropomorphic. God has revealed truths about himself to the human race, but always in ways that accommodate our human limitations.

GOD HAS REVEALED HIMSELF MOST FULLY IN CHRIST

Certainly, there's nothing more central to the Christian faith than Christ himself. He alone is our Savior and our Lord, and he is God's supreme revelation of himself to the human race. As Christ's followers, we acknowledge that God has revealed himself in many ways throughout biblical history, but passages like Colossians 1:15 tell us that Jesus is God's ultimate disclosure of himself in human terms. Jesus is the incarnate, eternal Son of God, the perfect human image and representative of God. For this reason, everything we believe about God must accord with God's supreme revelation in Jesus, in his teachings, as well as in the significance of his life, death, resurrection, ascension, and glorious return.

TYPES OF DIVINE REVELATION

More often than not, traditional systematic theologians identify two categories or types of divine revelation that Jesus himself acknowledged in his teachings. The first type is often called *general* or *natural revelation*.

General Revelation

General revelation, sometimes also called *natural revelation*, refers to the biblical teaching that God has revealed himself to human beings through their experiences of creation. In line with a number of Old Testament passages (Ps. 19, for example), Jesus himself frequently drew theological lessons from general revelation. He often referred to nature and common human activities, like farming and fishing, to teach about God. In fact, he repeatedly called on his disciples to look within and around themselves to discern what they could about God from their experiences of life.

We see something similar in passages like Acts 14:17 and 17:28. In these verses, the apostle Paul followed Christ's example and appealed to general revelation. Specifically, he pointed Gentiles toward what they knew about God through reflection on nature and Greek poetry.

We can't come to know God unless he reveals himself to us, and he does so in a number of ways: through creation and the wonders we see as we look around, in our relationships with other people who speak to us the things that they have learned about God, and, most important, in his holy Word, where God has revealed himself to us. We receive revelation from God on many different levels. We look around and we see God revealed to us; we know he exists. And then he tells us about himself through his disciples and his holy Word. **Jeffery Moore**

Romans 1–2 offers the most extensive explanation of general revelation in the Scriptures. These chapters draw attention to both positive and negative outlooks on general revelation that we must keep in view as we explore theology proper. On the positive side, Romans 1–2 teaches that human beings know many things about God through our experiences of life in God's creation. As the apostle Paul wrote, "God's invisible qualities—his eternal power and divine nature— have been clearly seen, being understood from what has been made" (Rom. 1:20). When we look closely at Romans 1–2, we see that "what has been made" is more than just the natural order. Paul also had in mind what is revealed about God through human culture, from human beings themselves, and even from our personal inner lives— our moral consciences, intuitions, premonitions, and the like.

General revelation is a really important theological concept because it's the one thing that cannot be denied. Christian or not, we're all living in the world God created. Now, whether or not a non-Christian acknowledges that is another story, but nonetheless we see a lot about who God is just by looking at creation. We see that we have a powerful God because he has created planets and stars and the moon. We have a God who has an eye for beauty—beautiful things matter to him, as we see in animals, in trees, in a sunset. We see the majesty of God in a lion. We see his character everywhere we look.

Now, this is very important, especially from an evangelistic point of view, because we need a starting point, and general revelation gives us that starting point. We know certain things about the world we live in, and therefore we know certain things about the God who created that world, by simply looking around us. **Ric Rodeheaver**

Throughout the centuries, this positive perspective on general revelation has played a major role in the doctrine of God in the form of "natural theology." Natural theology is the ongoing attempt to learn about God through careful reflection on general revelation. Followers of Christ have always recognized that we can learn a lot about God through natural theology. With rare exceptions, formal theological reflections on the doctrine of God in nearly every branch of the church have included natural theology.

In fact, leading Scholastic theologians during the medieval period constructed a formal, threefold strategy for pursuing natural theology. First, they spoke of "the way of causation" (*via causalitatis* in Latin). By this they meant that we can learn truths about God by observing the good things that God has created or "caused to be" in his creation. For instance, we can see that God created beauty and order in the world, so we may conclude that God himself must be beautiful and orderly.

Second, Scholastics spoke of "the way of negation" (*via negationis*). By this they meant that we can infer truths about God by contrasting him with the limitations and imperfections of creation. For instance, creation is limited by time, but God is eternal. Creation is limited by space, but God is infinite.

Third, medieval Scholastics also spoke of "the way of eminence" (*via eminentiae*). By this they meant that we can infer truths about God from general revelation by noting how God is always greater than the good things he has created. For example, the power of nature leads us to believe in the supreme power of God. Human intellectual abilities point us toward the incomparable wisdom of God.

For the most part, evangelicals today don't follow such rigorous methods, but natural theology continues to play a major role in theology proper. God designed every dimension of our experience of creation to reveal things about himself (Pss. 19:1–4; 97:6; Acts 14:17; 17:29; Rom. 1:19–20; 2:14–15). So, as his faithful people, we should be eager to search out everything we can learn about God through general revelation.

These positive outlooks on general revelation and natural theology are important to any study of theology proper, but we must also take into account that Romans 1–2 presents some crucial negative outlooks on the ways fallen human beings respond to general revelation. For example, Paul wrote, "The wrath of God is being revealed from heaven against all the godlessness and wickedness of men who suppress the truth by their wickedness" (Rom. 1:18).

In this verse, Paul explained that general revelation reveals "the wrath of God" rather than his mercy and salvation. This is true because, more often than not, sinful people "suppress the truth" of general revelation "by their wickedness." In fact, according to Romans 1:25, sinners have "exchanged the truth of God for a lie."

Jesus himself indicated time and again that sinful human beings frequently fail to learn what they should about God from their experiences of life. As Jesus and Paul both conveyed, sinful people have a propensity to lie to themselves and to others about what God has revealed through his creation.

God's creation teaches us a number of things. Most basically, of course, it teaches us that he is the sovereign Creator. God is the one who brings all things into being out of nothing; therefore, creation teaches us also about his power.

According to Romans 1, creation also teaches us about God's righteousness. Romans 1 tells us that all human beings know that there is a God and that he is to be worshiped. It tells us that we all have a sense of the righteousness and holiness of God, even though as sinful human beings, we suppress that knowledge and attempt to ignore it.

Creation teaches us that God is Creator, God is powerful, and God is righteous. We, as sinful human beings, attempt to deny and suppress those things. **Carl R. Trueman**

These perspectives raise a word of caution about relying too heavily on natural theology. Natural *revelation* is always true because it comes from God, but natural *theology* is fallible because sin has corrupted our ability to learn about God from our experiences of his creation. Despite the best efforts of sincere Christian theologians, natural theology has frequently misconstrued general revelation and introduced falsehoods into our concept of God.

For instance, during the patristic and medieval periods, Hellenistic mysticism led many to deny that human beings can rationally comprehend anything about God himself. In the eighteenth century, misunderstandings of the order of nature led a number of theologians to endorse Enlightenment deism—the belief that God is uninvolved in the affairs of the world. In recent centuries, scientific studies in biology have led many people to deny the biblical portrait of God as the Creator. At every turn, the corruption of the human heart has led theologians to miss the truth about God disclosed in general revelation.

These negative outlooks on natural theology lead to a fundamental question: If sin corrupts our awareness of general revelation, how can we know the truth about God? The answer, of course, is that we need special revelation, especially Scripture, to guide our interpretations of general revelation.

I would want to be very careful about what we can learn about God through the category of natural theology. Passages like Romans 1:20, which talk about God's majesty and power revealed in creation, give us something to hang our hats on. But we are in desperate need of special revelation to check human reasoning, since the created realm yields some things that can be read and understood problematically. Special revelation, which speaks of the reality of the Lord Jesus Christ, accurately fills in who God is. We desperately need to consult his Word to keep our reasoning in line. **Bruce L. Fields**

Special Revelation

Broadly speaking, *special revelation* is God's self-disclosure through supernatural means. The Holy Spirit has given revelation through dreams, visions, auditions, and through his great acts of salvation and judgment. God has also made himself known through inspired human representatives—his prophets and apostles who were inspired by the Holy Spirit. Of course, as we said earlier, God's greatest special revelation was in Christ.

The significance of special revelation for the doctrine of God hardly can be overstated. It is so essential to God's purposes that even before sin came into the world, God guided Adam and Eve through special verbal revelation, and, of course, special revelation has been critical after sin as well. It not only guides our attempts to understand general revelation, it also discloses the way of eternal salvation.

As wonderful as it is that God has granted supernatural revelation, both before and after sin came into the world, what we commonly call "special revelation from God" took place thousands of years ago. So, how do we learn about God through special revelation today?

Once again, we must turn to what Jesus, God's supreme revelation, taught. In brief, Christ taught his followers to devote themselves to God's special revelation in Scripture. Passages like Mark 12:28–34 clearly convey that Jesus, like other Palestinian rabbis in his day, affirmed the Old Testament as God's special written revelation.

The New Testament is also God's inspired revelation. In places like John 16:12–13 and Ephesians 2:20, we learn that after Jesus's ascension into heaven, he sent the Holy Spirit to equip his first-century apostles and prophets to reveal God to his church. The New Testament is our representative collection of these first-century apostolic and prophetic special revelations.

Divine revelation is the source of everything we know about God. Whether we're speaking of general or special revelation, God's self-disclosures are completely true and trustworthy. Still, evangelical Christians rightly insist that special revelation must always guide us as we seek to understand general revelation.

KEY TERMS AND CONCEPTS

divine revelation
general revelation
natural theology
special revelation
via causalitatis
via eminentiae
via negationis

REVIEW QUESTIONS

1. What is divine revelation?
2. In what four ways has God revealed himself in human terms (anthropomorphic revelation)?
3. What is general revelation?
4. How does God use general revelation to reveal himself to us?
5. What is special revelation?
6. How does God use special revelation to reveal himself to us?

DISCUSSION QUESTIONS

1. What attributes of God shown in the person of Jesus Christ most amaze you about your Creator?

2. How does the person of Jesus Christ prevent you from fashioning God into your image?
3. What kinds of things have you learned about the world around you from what God has revealed in nature apart from Scripture?
4. Has God's revelation through creation made a difference in your daily life?
5. How did God use his special revelation to bring you to a personal relationship with Jesus Christ as your Lord and Savior?
6. How should the importance of special revelation impact the way you minister to those around you?
7. How might you use general revelation to prove God's existence?

FOR FURTHER STUDY

Erickson, Millard. *Christian Theology*. Grand Rapids: Baker Book House, 1983.

Kline, Meredith G. *The Structure of Biblical Authority*. Grand Rapids: Eerdmans, 1972.

Kuyper, Abraham. *Principles of Biblical Authority*. Translated by J. H. de Vries. Grand Rapids: Eerdmans, 1968.

McDonald, H. D. *Theories of Revelation: An Historical Study, 1860–1960*. Grand Rapids: Baker Book House, 1979.

Vos, Geerhardus. *Biblical Theology: Old and New Testaments*. Grand Rapids: Eerdmans, 1948.

CHAPTER QUIZ

https://thirdmill.org/quiz?GOD1

2

DIVINE MYSTERIES

As we've seen, God has overcome the vast distance between himself and humanity. He has made it possible for us to know about him through his general and special revelation. At the same time, our knowledge of God is deeply affected by divine mysteries. There are many things that God has *not* revealed about himself.

We need to get a handle on who God really is, but that is not easy. He is transcendent—he's beyond the creation. He created all that we experience in this world. So, we can't really know him unless he reveals himself, unless he enters into creation somehow, unless he speaks to us, unless he reveals himself to us, which he has done most fully in his Son Jesus. His transcendence causes him to be mysterious to us. The only way we can know the kingdom of God, his reign and his rule, is if he reveals that to us.
Rick Boyd

The term *mystery* is used in a variety of ways in Scripture, but for our purposes, we may say that divine mysteries are the innumerable undisclosed truths about God that limit our understanding of God.

INNUMERABLE UNDISCLOSED
TRUTHS ABOUT GOD

The apostle Paul wrote that we should always be mindful of divine mysteries: "Oh, the depth of the riches of the wisdom and knowledge of God! How unsearchable his judgments, and his paths beyond tracing out!" (Rom. 11:33).

In the chapters leading up to Romans 11:33, Paul drew many true beliefs about God from both general and special revelation, but in this verse in particular, he pointed out the "depth" of God's wisdom and knowledge, and he accepted that God's judgments are "unsearchable" and "his paths [are] beyond tracing out." Paul was an authoritative apostle. He understood more about God through divine revelation than we can ever hope to understand, but even he faced countless mysteries—things that the Spirit of God had not revealed.

God is mysterious because he surpasses any comprehension or knowledge that we may have. Sometimes the way he acts is difficult for us to discern. He's also incomprehensible in the sense that no one can totally exhaust the knowledge of God. There is bound to be mystery because he is God and not a creature. If he weren't mysterious, we could safely say he wouldn't be God. Why would we want a God who isn't mysterious?

There is nothing about God's mysteriousness that is a problem for us in any ultimate way. The mystery of God doesn't mean he can't be accessed. It doesn't mean he doesn't love us and that we can't feel his love. We know him, not exhaustively, but we know him truly. We don't comprehend him, but we know him surely enough to say that we know God and not just some vague philosophical principle. **William Edgar**

Charles Hodge (1797–1878), the well-known professor of systematic theology at Princeton Theological Seminary, summed up divine mysteries in a remarkable way: "There is infinitely more in God than we have any idea of; and what we do know, we know imperfectly."[1] Hodge made two striking observations here. First, he insisted that what is true of God is "infinitely more . . . than we have any idea of." There are not just a handful of mysteries, nor even a great many mysteries. Rather, because God himself is infinite, there are infinitely more mysteries than we can even imagine. Second, Hodge also explained that even "what we do know [about God], we know imperfectly." In other words, there's not a single thing about God that we understand fully.

Sometimes when we hear someone say that God is incomprehensible, we react negatively: "Are you saying I can't come to know him?" Of course not. The Bible is God's self-revelation, after all. He has revealed himself so that we can come to know him in a personal way and that we can come to know something about him.

But if God is truly the infinite God, then my poor little mind, and even the best theological minds that have ever lived, will not be able to comprehend him in his fullness. By definition, if I could comprehend him, I would be as great as he is. Our God is not a little God. I cannot get all of him into my mind or into a book. We are grateful that he has provided for our salvation and that he has revealed enough of himself that we can come to some understanding of him and can live rightly in fellowship with him and can think rightly about him, though not exhaustively. **Gareth Cockerill**

LIMITATIONS OF OUR UNDERSTANDING

There are many different ways that divine mysteries limit what we know about God, but for our purposes here, we'll consider just two. On the one side, we have severely limited information about God. God has made clear what is essential for salvation and life in Christ, but in reality, none of us understands much about God. In

---

1. Charles Hodge, *Systematic Theology* (repr., Grand Rapids: Christian Classics Ethereal Library, 2005), 260.

1 Corinthians 13:12 we're told that we see only a "poor reflection" of the truth of God, as if we're looking "in a mirror."

In discussions of the doctrine of God, countless questions come up that simply can't be answered fully. For instance, why does God allow evil? How can we discern God's purposes in current events? Many theologians stray into speculation because they are afraid to admit that they don't have every answer to these kinds of questions. Yet divine mysteries should often lead Christ's faithful followers simply to admit, "I don't know." When it comes to the doctrine of God, if God hasn't revealed it, we can't know it. It's as simple as that. As faithful followers of Christ, we should never run from the fact that our knowledge of God is limited. In fact, it's a blessing to be reminded moment by moment of this limitation. Divine mysteries compel us to humble, childlike trust in God, even when we cannot understand him or his ways.

On the other side, human beings are only able to offer limited explanations of God's revelations. We're right to insist that the revelation of the God of truth doesn't contradict itself. There are many logical connections we can see among the revelations of God, but whether we admit it or not, divine mysteries limit our ability to explain the logical coherence of much of what God has revealed about himself.

For instance, we can't thoroughly explain the logic of the Trinity—the fact that God is one and three. Although the doctrine of the Trinity contains no logical fallacies or inconsistencies, there are still many mysteries that God hasn't revealed about his triune existence. In a similar way, we can't logically explain every dimension of the reality that Jesus is both truly God and truly man. Nor can we fully clarify how God can be entirely sovereign over human affairs and still hold us responsible for what we do. Throughout the centuries, the best Christian minds have rightly insisted that these biblical truths are logically consistent, but they haven't been able to provide anything close to complete explanations because they are beyond our comprehension.

Is it valuable to explain as much as we can about the logical coherence of what God has revealed about himself? Of course it is, but our ability to demonstrate logical coherence isn't our final standard of truth. The standard of truth is God's revelation. If God has revealed it, it's true, whether or not we can explain it satisfactorily.

> When theologians say that God is incomprehensible, they mean that his full essence and being cannot be grasped and understood by a finite being. Yet he has provided us with self-revelation that is adequate for us to come to faith. **Larry Cockrell**

TEMPORARY DIVINE MYSTERIES

It helps in many ways to distinguish two types of divine mysteries: temporary and permanent. On the one hand, temporary mysteries are truths about God that are hidden from human beings for a period of time, but then they are revealed at some later point in history. We all know that God often discloses things that were once mysterious as we gain more knowledge of general revelation. Our knowledge of God increases over time as we increase our understanding of the physical world, human cultures, other people, and ourselves.

Something similar is true with special revelation. Throughout the Scriptures, we find that some truths about God were hidden from God's people for a while and then revealed later. A careful reading of Scripture shows that God's later special revelations have never contradicted his earlier special revelations, but it also shows that God has disclosed more and more about himself over time. This unfolding of special revelation occurred at every period of biblical history. Of course, the most dramatic unveiling of divine mysteries took place in Christ. Paul had this in mind when he wrote Ephesians 1:9; 3:3; and 6:19. In these verses, Paul referred to the mystery of God's eternal purpose in Christ. He explained that this mystery had been kept hidden until the time of the New Testament apostles and prophets. For this reason, whenever we seek to learn about God, we must always search out later special revelation that clarifies tempo-rary mysteries found in earlier special revelation.

Sometimes we use the term *mysterious* to speak about God because we don't understand exactly what he's doing. The New Testament, however, generally uses the Greek word *mysterion* to mean that God's gracious plan of salvation is something that we would never have figured out on our own. That is, it's a mystery in the sense that we would never have understood it had God not revealed his plan to us in his special revelation. This is the rea-son that the word *mysterion* is used in Ephesians and 1 Corinthians. God is slowly unfolding his revelation and showing us how salvation is for both the Jew and the Gentile—for anyone who will accept Jesus Christ as the Mes-siah. **Samuel Lamerson**

Of course, we must also remember that, even as New Testament Christians, God hasn't revealed every temporary mystery to us just yet. As Paul wrote, "Now I know in part; then I shall know fully" (1 Cor. 13:12). Only when Christ returns in glory will he disclose every temporary mystery. Then, we will understand God and his ways far more fully than we do today.

Mystery in God is related specifically to his purposes and plans in creation—why does God work in this way and not that? There's a sense in which we can accept that God hasn't told us everything about himself—how could he? And how could we comprehend it? But he also hasn't told us every-thing about how he is working out his purposes and plans. Nobody knows that better than Job. When Job wanted an answer to his questions about why God allowed him to suffer, God didn't give him the answer he wanted. Instead he told him, "I know what I'm doing. There is a mystery to my plan that only I can fully explain and that you will see at the end of time when everything will suddenly and completely make sense." **Lewis Winkler**

PERMANENT DIVINE MYSTERIES

On the other hand, some divine mysteries are permanent rather than temporary. Permanent mysteries are truths about God that human beings will never grasp because these truths are beyond human comprehension. In traditional theology, this reality has led to the doctrine of the "incomprehensibility" of God. We can understand some things about God as he reveals them in human terms, but we'll never understand everything about anything about God. As God himself said, "For my thoughts are not your thoughts, neither are your ways my ways. . . . As the heavens are higher than the earth, so are my ways higher than your ways and my thoughts than your thoughts" (Isa. 55:8–9). In these verses, God reminded Israel that there were permanent mysteries because God and many of his ways are simply beyond our ability to comprehend.

We must always remember that, while God has revealed himself in both general and special revelation, God has also kept both temporary and permanent mysteries hidden from us. We simply cannot escape the reality that we are but creatures whose understanding of God is always severely limited.

When the Scriptures refer to God as mysterious, we have to make sure that we don't misunderstand the word *mystery*. When I think of things in this world as mysterious, I think that they have some dark secret that they will surprise me with at some point. That's not the case here. By *mysterious* we mean that God is incomprehensible. We mean that he has a life that is beyond our imagining. We mean that there is something about him that we cannot grasp entirely, and I quite like that. It means that he is beyond my creaturely life. He's greater than I could ever think. The technical theological word we use for this is *transcendence*. God is transcendent. He is beyond our scope of thinking—and that is why he is worthy of worship. That is why he is great. That is why we adore him. **Gary M. Burge**

KEY TERMS AND CONCEPTS

divine mysteries
incomprehensibility of God
permanent divine mysteries
temporary divine mysteries

REVIEW QUESTIONS

1. What do theologians mean when they talk about "divine mysteries"?
2. What are temporary divine mysteries? Give an example from Scripture.
3. What are permanent divine mysteries? Give an example from Scripture.

DISCUSSION QUESTIONS

1. How does the doctrine of God's transcendence comfort and reassure you in your Christian life?
2. What is it about God's complete "otherness" that challenges you most and why?
3. Name a few of God's actions that are difficult for you to understand.
4. What do you most look forward to understanding when Christ returns in glory?

FOR FURTHER STUDY

Bavinck, Herman. *The Doctrine of God*. Translated by William Hendriksen. London: Banner of Truth, 1978.

Bray, Gerald. *The Doctrine of God*. Downers Grove, IL: InterVarsity Press, 1993.

Flavel, John. *The Mystery of Providence*. 1677. Reprint, London: Banner of Truth, 1963.

Frame, John M. *The Doctrine of the Knowledge of God*. Phillipsburg, NJ: Presbyterian and Reformed, 1987.

CHAPTER QUIZ

https://thirdmill.org/quiz?GOD2

3

DIVINE ATTRIBUTES

At one time or another, most Christians have heard someone speak about the attributes of God. In later chapters, we'll explore God's attributes in some detail, but at this point we simply want to introduce the basic concept of divine attributes. What then are the attributes of God? If we were to ask most Christians this question, they would probably say that God's attributes are all the qualities or characteristics that the Scriptures attribute to God. This outlook is fine as far as it goes, but in traditional systematic theology the phrase *attributes of God* has a narrower, more technical meaning. Specifically, divine attributes are the perfections of God's essence revealed through a variety of historical manifestations.

PERFECTIONS OF GOD'S ESSENCE

This definition highlights two primary factors that characterize formal discussions of God's attributes. In the first place, God's attributes are the perfections of God's essence. Modern evangelicals don't often refer to God's essence. So, it will help to explore this concept a bit.

The word *essence* comes from the Latin term *essentia*, meaning "essence" or "being," which patristic and medieval theologians derived from the Greek word *ousia*—the word Neoplatonic and Aristotelian philosophers used to denote "being." Latin theology closely associated God's essence with his *substantia* or "substance." Now, Neoplatonists and Aristotelians approached the idea of essence in different ways, and there are a number of important complexities about the concept of essence that have been raised in modern philosophy, but the basic idea isn't difficult to grasp. In simple terms, the essence, being, or substance of something is the unchanging reality that underlies all of its outward, changing manifestations. Christian theologians have drawn upon this idea of essence as they've discussed the attributes or perfections of God.

Our discussion of God's essence will include four important distinctions: God's *essence* (what God is in himself); God's *perfections* or *attributes* (the qualities of God's essence); God's *long-term historical manifestations* (his disclosures of himself over long periods of time); and God's *short-term historical manifestations* (his disclosures of himself in relatively short periods of time).

To clarify what we mean by these terms, let's use the example of a human being. Imagine a person who is a soloist in church on Sundays; he's also a farmer who milks cows twice a day on his farm; he's a husband and a grandfather; and of course, as Christians, we know that he's the image of God, ordained as God's representative and God's servant. Some facts we know about this man refer to short-term historical manifestations of who he is. These things are true of him only now and then. He's a soloist in church, but only on Sundays. He milks cows, but only twice a day. While these descriptions are true of him, they don't refer to his essence. Rather, he remains the same man when he involves himself in these activities and when he doesn't.

Some of these descriptions refer to relatively long-term historical manifestations of who this man is. He's a husband and a grandfather for longer periods of time, but they are not essential to who the man is. He wasn't always a husband or a grandfather, but he was always the same man.

By contrast, when we speak of this man as the image of God, ordained to be God's representative and God's servant, we are speaking of permanent attributes that characterize his essence, qualities of his humanity. No matter what happens in his life, this description is true of him. Still, if we were to add up all that we know about this man, including his permanent attributes, we have not fully understood his essence. The essence of who this or any other man is remains somewhat elusive, always beyond our full grasp.

In many ways, systematic theologians make similar distinctions between God's essence, attributes, and long and short-term manifestations in history. Consider the first article of the Lutheran Augsburg Confession, written in 1530: "There is one Divine Essence which is called and which is God: eternal, without body, without parts, of infinite power, wisdom, and goodness, the Maker and Preserver of all things, visible and invisible."

As we see here, the Confession explicitly refers to the "one Divine Essence." This article resembles the discussions of God's essence found in the Anglican Thirty-Nine Articles of Religion and the Methodist Twenty-Five Articles of Religion. In effect, these documents affirm that the essence of God is the unchanging reality that underlies the variety of ways God has manifested himself.

Unfortunately, before the Reformation, many theologians who were inclined toward Christian mysticism followed Hellenistic philosophies and concluded that God's essence was completely shrouded in mystery. In this view, God's revelations tell us little, if anything, about his eternal essence. Rather, they only tell us about his secondary, changing, historical manifestations. Now, evangelicals agree that there is infinitely more to God's essence than we can know, but despite this, we still insist that God has actually revealed *some* of the attributes, or the qualities, of his divine essence. This belief clearly follows the teachings of Scripture.

Look again at the first article of the Augsburg Confession. Immediately after mentioning the "one Divine Essence," the Confession turns to a number of qualities or properties of God's essence. God is "eternal, without body, without parts, of infinite power, wisdom, and goodness." These attributes of God—these eternal, unchanging perfections—characterize God's essence.

On occasion, biblical authors referred explicitly to God's eternal, essential perfections. For instance, Psalm 34:8 declares that "the LORD is good," and Paul wrote in 1 Timothy 1:17 that God is "eternal." When we study all of Scripture, it's clear that no matter what God says or does in any situation, no matter what variety he displays, he is always good, and he is always eternal. The same kind of thing can be said regarding what the Scriptures teach about God's infinity, his holiness, his justice, his wisdom, his incomprehensibility, his omnipotence, and other divine attributes. These are all permanent qualities of his divine essence to which the Scriptures explicitly refer.

An attribute of God is that which is innate to God himself. It is that which makes him God. It is his nature, his substance. It is that reality in which Father, Son, and Holy Spirit all completely share. And so it's that which distinguishes God, in many respects, from what we are as finite creatures. It is what defines the "Godness" of God. **J. Scott Horrell**

REVEALED THROUGH HISTORICAL MANIFESTATIONS

The Scriptures occasionally refer directly to God's eternal attributes, but for the most part, they display God's attributes indirectly through descriptions, names and titles, metaphors and similes, and reports of his actions in history. None of these manifestations are contrary to his essence. God always manifests himself in ways that are true to who he is, but in systematic theology, God's attributes are not the same as his historical manifestations. Instead, we determine the attributes of God by asking, "What must always have been true of God, and what must always be true of God, that explains all the ways he has manifested himself in history?"

We have to be careful here. It usually isn't difficult to maintain this distinction between God's attributes and his manifestations when we deal with things that were true of God for relatively short periods of time. For instance, in Ezekiel 8:18, God said that he would not listen to the prayers of his people, but clearly, we shouldn't conclude that it's God's essence to refuse to listen to prayers. In many other places, the Scriptures tell us that God does listen to prayers. Both of these descriptions of God are true historical manifestations of who he is at particular times, but neither is a quality of his essence. Instead, God's attributes are the eternal perfections of his essence that are true of him both when he listens and when he does not listen to prayers.

By contrast, it's often more difficult to distinguish between God's attributes and his historical manifestations when they last for relatively long periods of time. For example, we may be tempted to think that patience is an attribute of God because he has shown patience toward sinners generation after generation. Yet, as we know from the Bible, God's patience ends with different people at different times in history, and it will end for all sinners at the final judgment when Christ returns in glory. So, in the technical sense of systematic theology, even something as long-lasting as divine patience is not an eternal attribute of God's essence.

We'll explore this distinction in more detail in later chapters, but at this point the basic idea should be clear. God manifests himself in short-term and long-term ways in history, but the attributes of God are those qualities that have always been true of him and that will continue to be true of him forever.

TYPES OF DIVINE ATTRIBUTES

Because the Bible doesn't explicitly identify all of God's attributes, and because it doesn't classify them for us, theologians have grouped God's perfections in different ways. Many scholars have classified God's attributes along the lines we mentioned in chapter 1: "the way of causation," "the way of negation," and "the way of eminence." Another common way of classifying God's attributes is based on current understandings of human beings as the image of God. In this approach, it's common to speak of God's perfections as his "intellect," "will," and "moral character." Neither of these systems of classification have been the most prominent in the history of Christian theology, but we need to keep them in mind because they appear time and again, either explicitly or implicitly, as theologians discuss the attributes of God.

For the most part, evangelicals have favored dividing God's perfections into two main types of attributes: incommunicable and communicable. Well-known theologians have often pointed out the limitations of this twofold classification, and we'll look into some of these limitations in the chapters that follow, but this distinction continues to be a common and helpful way of speaking of the perfections of God's essence.

Incommunicable Attributes

The term *incommunicable* means "unable to be shared." God's incommunicable attributes are those perfections of his essence that creation—including human beings as the image of God—cannot share with him. As such, incommunicable attributes roughly correspond to the perfections of God that we determine through the "way of negation." These attributes focus on how God is different from his creation.

As we saw earlier in this chapter, the first article of the Augsburg Confession refers to six attributes of God. He is "eternal, without body, without parts, of infinite power, wisdom, and goodness." Although it's something of an oversimplification, it's common for the incommunicable attributes of God to be associated with the terms "eternal," "without body," and "without parts," as well as with the adjective "infinite." God is eternal; we are temporal. He is without body; we are corporeal. He is without parts; we are divided into parts. He is infinite; we are finite.

For God to communicate with us in human terms, the Scriptures occasionally draw upon faint, positive comparisons between these incommunicable attributes and creation. Yet without a doubt, the primary way the Bible explains these attributes of God is through contrast between God and his creation. As a result, the Scriptures don't call on human beings to imitate God in these ways. We aren't instructed to try to be eternal, without bodies, without parts, or infinite. On the contrary, the Scriptures call on us to acknowledge these attributes of God in humble worship and praise because he is so different from us.

Communicable Attributes

The term *communicable* signifies that something is able to be shared. God's communicable attributes are those perfections of his essence that creation—especially human beings as the image of God—can share with him. Of the attributes listed in the first article of the Augsburg Confession, God's communicable attributes are usually associated with "power," "wisdom," and "goodness." God possesses these to an infinite degree, but human beings also have power, wisdom, and goodness. We possess them imperfectly and on a human scale, but we possess them nonetheless.

It's important for students of systematic theology to understand the difference between the communicable and incommunicable attributes of God, because we've got to understand what makes us different from God. God is wholly other, distinct from his creation, yet we are created in the image of God, and although we are finite and changeable and mutable, certain aspects of our being are like God's. We can have knowledge. We can love. We can seek justice and mercy. Many things that God does perfectly, we do in a finite level. **Brandon P. Robbins**

The primary way that we understand God's communicable attributes is by comparison. In this sense, the communicable attributes roughly correspond to those that medieval Scholastic theologians identified through "the way of causation" and "the way of eminence." Throughout Scripture, we're often commanded not simply to admire these divine attributes, but also to imitate them. We're to be more and more like God in our exercise of power, and we're to imitate him by developing and displaying wisdom and goodness in our lives.

KEY TERMS AND CONCEPTS

communicable attributes
divine attributes
essence of God
historical manifestations
incommunicable attributes

REVIEW QUESTIONS

1. What does the theological term *essence* mean?
2. How do systematic theologians define divine attributes?
3. What are historical manifestations of divine attributes?
4. Why must we carefully distinguish between God's attributes and his historical manifestations?
5. What are incommunicable divine attributes? Give an example.
6. What are communicable divine attributes? Give an example.

DISCUSSION QUESTIONS

1. If God's perfections weren't permanent, how would that impact your view of him?
2. How would you handle historical manifestations of God's perfections that appeared to reveal contradictory things about God's essence?
3. How can you gain confidence that you've properly understood the things God has revealed about himself through historical manifestations?
4. If God's incommunicable attributes aren't clearly revealed through historical manifestations, how much can we really know about them?
5. In what specific ways do you personally need to change in order to be more like God?

FOR FURTHER STUDY

Bavinck, Herman. *Reformed Dogmatics*. Edited by John Bolt. Translated by John Vriend. 4 vols. Grand Rapids: Baker Academic, 2003–8.

Berkhof, Louis. *Systematic Theology*. New ed. Grand Rapids: Eerdmans, 1996.

Erickson, Millard J. *Christian Theology*. Grand Rapids: Baker Book House, 1983.

Kaiser, Christopher B. *The Doctrine of God*. Westchester, IL: Good News, 1982.

Packer, J. I. *Knowing God*. London: Hodder and Stoughton, 1973.

CHAPTER QUIZ

https://thirdmill.org/quiz?GOD3

4

DIVINE WORKS

If we were to ask most evangelicals, "What are the works of God?" most of us would simply point to those places where the Scriptures say that God did this or that. This answer would be right, as far as it goes, but systematic theologians approach divine works much like they approach divine attributes. Instead of focusing on specific historical events, they seek to understand what lies behind these events. They ask, "What can we know that is always true of what God has done, is doing, and will do?" We can summarize this basic approach by saying that the topic of divine works refers to how God works all things according to his eternal purposes.

GOD WORKS ALL THINGS

The idea that divine works include every event that occurs in history often seems a bit theoretical and speculative for new students of theology, so we should say a few words about this dimension of the works of God. Let's begin with how Paul described God as "him who works out everything in conformity with the purpose of his will" (Eph. 1:11). It's unusual for modern evangelicals to think about God's works on such a large scale. For many of us, we read the Scriptures and conclude that only some things that occur in history are works of God. In contrast to this point of view, Paul believed that God has a hand in every single event that ever has occurred and ever will occur.

To be sure, Scripture speaks of both divine and creaturely causes of historical events. Sometimes the Bible speaks of God acting in the world, such as when he delivered Israel at the Red Sea. At other times, it refers to preternatural creatures causing events to occur, such as when Satan tempted Job to curse God. Beyond this, we read about human beings causing things to happen, such as when David made preparations for Solomon's temple. In addition, we read of animals and plants having effects on events as well, and the Bible also talks of inanimate objects, like the sun, influencing what happens in history.

In light of these differentiations, the question in traditional Christian theology is, should we limit what we call "God's works" simply to those events that Scripture attributes exclusively to God? Over the centuries, evangelical theologians have responded to this question with a resounding no.

Drawing terminology from Aristotle, systematic theologians have described God as the "First Cause" of all things. Now, this does not mean that God, as the First Cause, simply began history. Rather, God is the ultimate cause behind every event that occurs at every moment. Even so, systematic theologians have also spoken of *second* causes. Second causes are created beings or objects that perform real but secondary roles in causing events to occur.

This distinction between the First Cause and second causes is based on the fact that the Scriptures treat more than just a handful of spectacular, miraculous events—like the deliverance of Israel at the Red Sea—as divine works. The first chapter of Job makes it clear that God commissioned Satan to test Job. In 1 Chronicles 29:16 David gave God the glory for his successful preparations for Solomon's temple. Passages like Psalm 147:7–9 indicate that God is in control of what animals and plants do. In addition, the effects of inanimate objects, like the sun, are attributed to God in passages like Isaiah 45:6–7.

In a later chapter, we'll explore how God, the First Cause, employs creation, or second causes, in a variety of ways. In particular, we'll see how this helps us understand that God is not the author of evil. For now, however, we simply want to point out that, in one way or another, God's works include everything that occurs in history, whether he does them directly or indirectly.

GOD WORKS ACCORDING TO HIS PURPOSE

Theologians have also given a lot of attention to how God's works occur according to his eternal, unchanging plan or purposes. Now, it's fair to say that many modern evangelicals are unfamiliar with this concept, and those who speak of such matters have different ways of understanding them. So we should take a moment to explain the basic idea that we have in mind.

In Ephesians 1:11, Paul said that God works all things "in conformity with the purpose of his will." Here, Paul referred to the Old Testament concept that God has an eternal plan for history—a plan that he is sure to fulfill. For instance, in Isaiah 46:10 God said, "I make known the end from the beginning, from ancient times, what is still to come. I say: My purpose will stand, and I will do all that I please."

This facet of God's works is so mysterious that faithful Christians have understood it in many different ways, but on the whole, we have always affirmed that God has an eternal plan. In addition, his works—which include every dimension of history—always fulfill his eternal purposes. God is not ignorant of what will happen in history. He is never surprised by history. His purposes are not frustrated. As mysterious as it is, nothing is beyond God's all-encompassing plan for history in Christ.

Whenever something happens in the world, people wonder, "Is this something that God had in mind or not?" Particularly when things go wrong in the world, we wonder, "Where is God in this, and what is his purpose?" It's helpful for us to understand the fullness of the biblical doctrine of the sovereignty of God because it's clear that nothing that happens is outside the ultimate will and purpose of God. We can point to lots of places in Scripture that show this. Ephesians 1, for example, says that God works out everything according to the purpose of his will, and so everything that has ever happened in history is ultimately part of the purposes of God. This is a great mystery for us with our limited minds. **Philip Ryken**

If God is omniscient, if God's knowledge is comprehensive of the past, present, and future, all things possible and all things actual, then all historical events are part of his plan. **Glenn R. Kreider**

TYPES OF DIVINE WORKS

Formal discussions of the doctrine of God often distinguish between different types or kinds of divine works. As just one example, let's take another look at the first article of the Augsburg Confession. It says: "There is one Divine Essence which is called and which is God: eternal, without body, without parts, of infinite power, wisdom, and goodness, the Maker and Preserver of all things, visible and invisible."

The Confession draws attention to two types of divine works. On the one side, it mentions that God is "the Maker . . . of all things, visible and invisible." On the other side, it mentions that God is the "Preserver of all things, visible and invisible." These affirmations represent a prominent, traditional distinction between two types of divine works: creation and providence.

Creation

God's work of creation is easy to recognize. We all know that the Bible begins with the words, "In the beginning God created the heavens and the earth" (Gen. 1:1). In many respects, the Scriptures begin with this teaching because it forms the basis of everything we believe about the works of God.

There are many ways to summarize traditional treatments of God's work of creation in theology proper, but at this point, it will suffice to mention three main emphases: the *fact* of creation (God created everything that exists); the *variety* of creation (God created variety both in the physical and spiritual realms); and the *purpose* of creation (God established the creation to fulfill his eternal purposes).

Providence

God's work of providence is his work of preserving his creation. Unfortunately, evangelical Christians today don't often realize how profound God's work of providence is. They imagine that when God created the world, he gave it a measure of independence so that it can hold together without his attention, but in traditional systematic theology, the term *providence*—from the Latin term *providentia*—has connotations of "attending to something" or "taking care of something." This terminology reflects the Christian belief that creation is just as dependent on God now as it was at the very first moment of creation.

Paul wrote, "By [Christ] all things were created: things in heaven and on earth, visible and invisible, whether thrones or powers or rulers or authorities; all things were created by him and for him. He is before all things, and in him all things hold together" (Col. 1:16–17). As this passage indicates, not only is it true that in Christ all things were created, it's equally true that in him all things hold together. By drawing this parallel, the apostle made it clear that creation would simply fall apart if it weren't for God's providence—his preserving and sustaining care—constantly working in creation.

Much like the work of creation, the work of providence can be summarized in three main ways: the *fact* of God's providential care for creation (God preserves and sustains everything he has made); the *variety* of God's providential care (God interacts with different facets of creation in different ways); and the *purpose* of God's providential care (God ensures that creation will fulfill his eternal purposes). As we continue to study the doctrine of God, we'll see more clearly how crucial it is to understand the works of God, both his work of creation and his work of providence.

> The providence of God is God's ongoing care for his creation and all his creatures. Through his Word, through his Spirit, God continues to sustain the world. He provides what we need—food, water, air. He provides all the things we take for granted. As the governor, he oversees all events, even historic events that we may be mystified by. We believe God is in charge and guiding these events to his own outcome, providing for us and for our salvation, helping us to realize our need for his gracious work of restoration. He, as the great heavenly Father who loves us so much, provides us every good gift that we need to sustain us. **Justyn Terry**

All followers of Christ should be eager to grow in their personal knowledge of God and in their experience of his actions in the world, but to do this we must also devote ourselves to learning as much as we possibly can about God. In this opening section, we've introduced a few of the main issues that come to the foreground in theology proper. As we continue in the chapters that follow, we'll learn more about the doctrine of God as we explore who God is and what he does. In this way, we'll see how increasing our knowledge of God is essential to every dimension of Christian theology and to every dimension of faithful service to God.

KEY TERMS AND CONCEPTS

creation
divine works
First Cause
God's eternal plan
providence
second causes

REVIEW QUESTIONS

1. How do evangelicals define divine works?
2. What does it mean that God "works out everything in conformity with the purpose of his will" (Eph. 1:11)?
3. What does it mean when we say that God is the maker of all things?
4. What does it mean when we say that God is the preserver of all things?

DISCUSSION QUESTIONS

1. What does God's work of creation imply about his purpose for creation?
2. How might the doctrine of providence reassure and strengthen you when you suffer trials or face temptations?
3. How might you use the doctrine of providence to reassure and strengthen others?
4. When have you been most tempted to think that God is not at work in your life? How might a biblical understanding of God's work help you overcome that temptation?

FOR FURTHER STUDY

Berkouwer, G. C. *The Providence of God*. Translated by Lewis B. Smedes. Studies in Dogmatics. Grand Rapids: Eerdmans, 1952.

Frame, John M. *The Doctrine of God*. Phillipsburg, NJ: P&R Publishing, 2002.

Gilkey, Langdon. *Maker of Heaven and Earth : A Study of the Christian Doctrine of Creation*. Garden City, NY: Doubleday, 1959.

Helm, Paul. *The Providence of God*. Downers Grove, IL: InterVarsity Press, 1994.

Hodge, Charles. *Systematic Theology*. Reprint, Grand Rapids: Christian Classics Ethereal Library, 2005.

CHAPTER QUIZ

https://thirdmill.org/quiz?GOD4

PART TEST

https://thirdmill.org/quiz?GOD1s

PART 2

HOW GOD IS
DIFFERENT FROM US

A young man was taking his friend to hear a new musician in town. "You're going to love this guy," he assured his companion.

"Who is he like?" his friend asked.

The young man replied with excitement in his voice, "He's not like anyone you've ever heard before. You'll be amazed at how different he is."

We've all had experiences like this. There are always ways in which people we admire are like others, but these commonalities usually don't catch our attention. More often than not, what makes us admire them most is how different they are from others. In many ways, the same kind of thing is true about God. Every faithful follower of Christ honors and worships God for all that he is and all that he does, but what frequently lifts our spirits in amazement is how gloriously different God is from everything he has created.

5

IDENTIFYING GOD'S INCOMMUNICABLE ATTRIBUTES

In a previous chapter, we defined divine attributes as the perfections of God's essence revealed through a variety of historical manifestations. In other words, God's attributes are those qualities of his essence without which he'd no longer be God. We saw that theologians have commonly spoken of two main types, or classes, of God's attributes. His *communicable* attributes are those qualities of God's essence that creation can share in limited ways. His *incommunicable* attributes are those qualities of God's essence that creation cannot share. In this section, we'll concentrate on the second of these classes: God's incommunicable attributes.

When we talk about who God is and what Scripture reveals to us about who God is—what people call the attributes of God—we describe his attributes as communicable or incommunicable. Why is that distinction important? It's important because it helps us to understand who God is—God is distinct. Think about a word like *aseity*, which means that God exists only by making himself exist. In other words, he depends on nothing, whereas we depend on him for our existence. There's something very different about God. So the distinction between incommunicable and communicable attributes not only helps us to know who God is but also helps us to know how God is God and we are not. **Vincent Bacote**

General revelation gives us many insights into God's incommunicable attributes when we contrast the qualities of God's essence with the qualities of his creation. Medieval Scholastics called this strategy *via negationis*, or "the way of negation." Yet we must always remember that God has given his people special revelation to guide us as we reflect on what general revelation teaches about God's incommunicable attributes. This means that followers of Christ today must always consider what the Scriptures teach as we seek to identify God's incommunicable attributes.

BIBLICAL FOUNDATION

During the patristic and medieval periods, Hellenistic philosophies deeply influenced theology proper. These philosophies emphasized that God is transcendent and, therefore, utterly removed from history. Under this influence, Christian theologians easily recognized the incommunicable attributes of God on nearly every page of Scripture. Yet in the modern period, many influential critical theologians, and even a number of evangelicals, have turned from these Hellenistic influences. As a result, they've focused primarily on what the Scriptures reveal about God's immanence—his involvement in history. For this reason, it's quite common for many sincere Christians today to downplay, and even deny, that the Bible supports the traditional doctrine of God's incommunicable attributes. Because of these doubts, it's important for us to stress that biblical authors and characters often referred to the fact that God is incomparable, matchless, without equal, and utterly supreme.

For example, Solomon praised God at the dedication of the temple in this way: "O Lord, God of Israel, there is no God like you in heaven above or on earth below" (1 Kings 8:23). Notice how Solomon's declaration about God's incomparability is without exception. There is no other god anywhere who is like him (see also Pss. 71:19; 86:8; 89:6).

Similarly, Solomon's father, David, proclaimed, "How great you are, O Sovereign Lord! There is no one like you, and there is no God but you" (2 Sam. 7:22). As we see here, David spoke about God's incomparability in a way that revealed what it means to be God. David explicitly said that God is unlike everyone else, but he also claimed that the Sovereign Lord, "the Lord, Yahweh" (*'ădōnāy yhwh* in Hebrew), is so great that he is the only God. In other words, God's incomparability is essential to what makes him God (see also Job 40–41; Isa. 40–46).

These and similar passages establish the biblical foundation that justifies a careful study of God's incommunicable perfections. They exemplify the consistent biblical teaching that God is beyond all comparisons with his creation. This facet of theology proper has been called into question in some circles and dramatically minimized in others, but Scripture emphasizes God's incomparability, and his incomparability calls on us to learn all we can about how God is different from his creation.

THEOLOGICAL VARIETY

Evangelicals don't always agree on how to identify and define God's incommunicable attributes. One reason for our different outlooks is that the Scriptures don't give us anything close to a complete, authoritative list of these attributes. Instead, teachings on these matters appear in various places and ways throughout the Bible. As a result, identifying God's incommunicable perfections is similar to constructing intricately designed stained-glass windows out of shapes and hues that appear in different parts of the Bible. As you can imagine, there are many complex processes that go into identifying these shapes and colors, synthesizing what we find, and cataloging them. We certainly hold many outlooks in common, but it shouldn't surprise us that evangelicals have created different lists of God's incommunicable attributes.

Historical Documents

We can gain a sense of this theological variety by looking at three historical documents from different branches of the Protestant church: the Augsburg Confession (1530), the Belgic Confession (1561), and the Westminster Shorter Catechism (1647).

Augsburg Confession. Earlier, we noted how the first article of the Lutheran Augsburg Confession summarizes God's attributes in this way: "There is one Divine Essence which is called and which is God: eternal, without body, without parts, of infinite power, wisdom, and goodness." This article speaks of six divine perfections. It has been common to identify God's eternality, lack of a body, lack of parts, and infinity as incommunicable attributes. These are ways in which God is different from his creation.

Belgic Confession. The Reformed Belgic Confession represents another perspective on God's incommunicable attributes. In its first article, it says: "There is one only simple and spiritual Being, which we call God. . . . He is eternal, incomprehensible, invisible, immutable, infinite, almighty, perfectly wise, just, good, and the overflowing fountain of all good."

Along with noting that God is a spiritual Being (based on Jesus's words in John 4:24), the Belgic Confession describes God with ten other terms. By and large, theologians have treated God's simplicity (meaning he's not divided into parts), eternality, incomprehensibility, invisibility, immutability (or unchangeableness), and infinity as incommunicable attributes.

Westminster Shorter Catechism. Finally, let's consider the Westminster Shorter Catechism. It responds to question 4, "What is God?" by saying, "God is a Spirit, infinite, eternal, and unchangeable, in his being, wisdom, power, holiness, justice, goodness, and truth." Like the Belgic Confession, this catechism describes God as a Spirit and then lists ten divine perfections. It's common to speak of God's infinity, eternality, and unchangeableness (or immutability) as incommunicable attributes.

Conceptual Agreement

When we set these lists of God's incommunicable attributes alongside each other, we see that they are not the same. All three documents mention that God is eternal and infinite, but only the Belgic Confession and the Shorter Catechism state that God is a spiritual Being or a Spirit and that God is immutable or unchangeable. Only the Augsburg Confession claims that God is without body and without parts, and only the Belgic Confession says that God is simple, incomprehensible and invisible. As we can see from these comparisons, evangelicals have expressed God's incommunicable attributes in different ways, but how substantial are these differences?

When theological students first learn that evangelicals don't all use precisely the same terminology for God's incommunicable attributes, they often assume that we believe very different things about God. As in every facet of systematic theology, it's true that variations among us often represent different theological emphases, but more often than not, differences in our lists of God's incommunicable attributes represent little more than variety in technical terminology. Although faithful followers of Christ have used different technical terms to list God's incommunicable attributes, by and large, these differences don't represent substantial disagreements.

As we've just noted, the Augsburg Confession mentions that God is without body. Although the Belgic Confession and the Westminster Shorter Catechism don't use this expression, they still convey the same belief or concept.[1] The Belgic Confession touches

---

1. The Westminster Confession of Faith and Larger Catechism reflect similar variety.

on this when it says that God is a spiritual Being and invisible, and in a similar way the Shorter Catechism affirms that God is a Spirit.[2]

The Augsburg Confession also states that God is without parts. The Belgic Confession says the same thing when it describes God as simple. This is an older way of saying "undivided" or "without parts." The Westminster Shorter Catechism covers this attribute when it says that God is infinite. He has no parts because his perfections have no limits.

Similarly, only the Belgic Confession says that God is incomprehensible, but the Augsburg Confession and the Westminster Shorter Catechism imply this divine attribute by their use of the term "infinite." Because God's mind is without limits, we cannot comprehend him.

Clearly, evangelicals have cataloged the incommunicable attributes of God using different *terms*, but by and large our *concepts* of God aren't significantly different. So, as we explore God's incommunicable attributes, we should always look beyond particular technical terms and focus on the concepts or beliefs that they signify.

When theologians do their work, or when believers come together to build confessions to describe the beliefs and theology of the church, they're trying to describe the same reality, but they may make different choices. It shouldn't be a surprise that when we start talking about something so immense and so important, we may use different words. We need to seek what underlying reality the words are trying to describe and to compare those things.

What can be more confusing is when two different groups of people use the same word to describe two very different things. Then we can't just put the words next to each other. Rather, we have to dig behind the words to find out what those theologians or those authors of the confessions are trying to describe. We have to take what sits underneath the words and compare it to see where there is and isn't difference. Very often, when we do this task, we discover less difference than we expected because these confessions are rooted in the authority of Scripture and the work of Christ.

2. See also the Westminster Confession of Faith, chapter 2.1.

Even if they use different words to describe that one reality, they're still aimed at the same thing. **Tim Sansbury**

This is especially important when we realize that other terms have been used for these attributes as well. For instance, theologians commonly refer to the *omnipresence* of God (the fact that God is everywhere), the *omniscience* of God (the fact that he knows everything), and the *omnipotence* of God (the fact that God is all-powerful). Many theologians also speak of the *aseity* of God (the fact that God is self-sufficient and independent from his creation) and the *sovereignty* of God (the fact that God is in total control of creation). To be sure, there are disagreements over some details of what these incommunicable perfections mean, but for the most part, they don't represent major differences of opinion among well-informed evangelical theologians.

DIVINE TRANSCENDENCE

It's one thing to come up with a list of terms to describe how God is different from his creation. It's another thing to identify these terms with the many relevant teachings of Scripture. God's incommunicable attributes are some of the most abstract concepts in Christian theology, so if we hope to avoid serious misunderstandings, we have to account for a broad range of biblical perspectives. One way to clarify the breadth of biblical teachings on God's incommunicable attributes is to focus on what has often been called *divine transcendence*. Simply put, when we speak of divine transcendence, we mean that God isn't restricted by the limitations he established for his creation. He's above and beyond creation.

Transcendence involves the concept of "above and beyond," so when we talk about the transcendence of God, we're thinking of God as bigger than and above the merely human. To talk about divine transcendence is to describe God as inherently, in his nature, God—not an idol, not a god who is maneuvered by humans or magically manipulated, but *God*. This means that as we think through who God is, we must accept that he is actually God and therefore worthy of worship. This great, enormous God, the Creator, the master of time and space, is above and beyond his creation and above and beyond the manipulation of humans. **Josh Moody**

Biblical Concepts

You'll recall that question and answer 4 of the Westminster Shorter Catechism speak of God as infinite, eternal, and unchangeable. Each of these terms summarizes many biblical teachings on God's transcendence.

Infinite. Christians are often surprised to learn that the word *infinite* doesn't appear in many translations of the Bible. Rather, it's a philosophical term for a concept that the Scriptures express in a variety of ways. Our English term *infinite* translates two Latin theological terms: *immensus* (meaning "immeasurable" or "incalculable") and *infinitus* (meaning "unending" or "unlimited"). When we say that God is infinite, we mean he is immeasurable, incalculable, unending, and unlimited. Simply put, God's perfections are without limits.

A number of biblical passages rather explicitly refer to different ways in which God is infinite. For example, Solomon indicated that God cannot be limited by space when he declared to God, "even the highest heaven, cannot contain you" (1 Kings 8:27). Paul indicated that God's knowledge and wisdom can't be measured when he spoke of God's "unsearchable . . . judgments, and his paths [that are] beyond tracing out" (Rom. 11:33). The psalmist said that God is so great that knowledge of him is "too wonderful . . . too lofty . . . to attain" (Ps. 139:6). These and similar passages indicate that it is right to speak of God as infinite in his perfections.

God's infinity is a way of speaking about God's unlimitedness. We live in the coordinates of time and space—two coordinates that are difficult to talk about in the abstract—and when we speak of God's infinity, we're trying to communicate that God is not bounded in the same way we are by time and space. To talk about God's temporal existence or spatial existence is a kind of misuse of categories. God in one sense is "outside time"—but even then we're using spatial language to talk about time. Fundamentally, to speak of God's infinity is to say God is not limited in the ways we are limited. **Richard Lints**

Eternal. Our English word *eternal* often translates the Hebrew terms *'ad, 'ôlām,* and occasionally *naṣaḥ* in the Old Testament, and the Greek terms *aiōn* and *aiōnios* in the Greek translation of the Old Testament (the Septuagint) and in the New Testament. From time to time, these terms are also applied to facets of creation, but not in the same sense as they are applied to God. When theologians speak of God's *eternality,* they refer to the fact that creation is temporal—limited by time in many different ways—but God is not. God is eternal in the sense that God's perfections are not restricted by time in any way.

A number of biblical passages speak of the eternality of God. For instance, 1 Timothy 1:17 speaks of the eternal rule of God when it says, "Now to the King eternal . . . the only God, be honor and glory for ever and ever." Revelation 4:8 praises God as eternal when the heavenly creatures call him the one "who was, and is, and is to come." And 2 Peter 3:8 speaks of how God transcends all of history when it says, "With the Lord a day is like a thousand years, and a thousand years are like a day." These and many similar passages indicate that time does not restrict God's attributes in any way. His perfections are eternal.

The Bible often speaks of God as eternal—from everlasting to everlasting. That means there was no beginning when there wasn't a God or when God did not exist. Creation is not eternal. The entire universe had a beginning. God created the heavens and the earth out of nothing, but God does not have a beginning. God has been from eternity without end, and God is God forever, from everlasting to everlasting. *Eternal* means there's no time when God does not exist, either in the past or in the future. **Paul R. Raabe**

Unchangeable. There are a number of biblical expressions that indicate that God is unchangeable. The Hebrew verb *šānâ* means "change." The Hebrew verb *nāṣam* means "change one's mind." And the Greek noun *parallagē* means "change" or "variation." Common experience and the Bible indicate that everything in creation is, at some level, changeable, but when these kinds of terms are applied to God's attributes, they speak of another way in which God is amazingly different from his creation. According to the Bible, God's perfections cannot change.

God himself said he was unchangeable in Malachi 3:6. In this verse, God contrasted his own constancy with the instability of Israel's loyalty by stating, "I the LORD do not change." Numbers 23:19 contrasts God with human beings by saying, "God is not a man . . . that he should change his mind." In addition, James assured his audience of God's consistency by describing him as "the Father of the heavenly lights, who does not change like shifting shadows" (James 1:17). These and similar passages depict God as one who is immutable or unchangeable.

God doesn't change. The Bible specifically says this in many places, but most obviously in Hebrews 13:8: "Jesus Christ is the same yesterday and today and forever." For example, the Bible doesn't indicate that God, over time, softens or lowers the standards of his law. He never looks at the human race and says, "I knew they weren't perfect, but now I see how *really* imperfect they are, so I won't require them to live up to the same standards." What

God told Moses on Mount Sinai and what God has revealed throughout the Scriptures remain the same standard for us. This would be very frightening if it were not for the fact that the gospel message doesn't change either. God has always loved his creation and specifically, very purposefully, loved human beings enough that he came into the world to make a difference in our lives so that we wouldn't be consigned to hell forever but could live with him in heaven forever. God's immutability is a warning to us on the one side and a great comfort to us on the other. **Jeffery Moore**

Theological Misconceptions

When we consider both general revelation and the Scriptures, it's difficult to deny that God transcends his creation in all three ways we've mentioned. Creation is finite, but God is infinite. Creation is temporal, but God is eternal. Creation is changeable, but God is unchangeable. Still, the terms *infinite*, *eternal*, and *unchangeable* are so abstract that they easily can be misconstrued. Many theologians have wrongly inferred that these incommunicable attributes form an impenetrable barrier between God and his creation. Despite many rather obvious teachings to the contrary in both Scripture and systematic theology, these theologians conclude that because God is infinite, eternal, and unchangeable, he cannot actually enter into and engage the finite, temporal, and changing creation.

Many mistakenly argue, for instance, that because God has infinite knowledge, he never investigates circumstances; however, the Scriptures frequently speak to the contrary. For instance, in Genesis 18:20–21, God sent angelic spies to investigate the sin of Sodom and Gomorrah.

Similarly, the fact that God is eternal has led many to conclude that God never waits to react to human obedience and disobedience, but the Scriptures speak this way about God frequently. For example, Deuteronomy 8:2 tells us that God waited to judge Israel in the exodus until after they had failed their tests of obedience.

In addition, the truth that God is unchangeable has led some well-meaning Christians to conclude that God never actually responds to human actions like prayer; however, God responds to prayer throughout the Bible. As just one example, after God declared that he was going to destroy the Israelites at the foot of Mount Sinai (Ex. 32:14), God responded to Moses's prayer and relented from destroying his people.

Unfortunately, all too often, evangelicals stray toward deism by concluding that biblical references to God's engagements with his creation are mere "appearances." From this point of view, God who is infinite, eternal, and unchangeable doesn't actually involve himself with his creation; it only *seems* as if he does. In reality, the terms *infinite*, *eternal*, and *unchangeable* indicate the opposite. Because God is free from the limitations of creation, he is able to— and does—enter the finite, temporal, changing world in any way he wishes.

When we conceive of God's incommunicable attributes in ways that diminish the reality of his involvement with creation, we strike at the heart of biblical faith. What could be more important in Scripture than the fact that God is fully and genuinely engaged with his finite, temporal, and changing creation? What could be more important to all of us than the reality that God interacts with us?

DIVINE IMMANENCE

To avoid these sorts of misconceptions about God's incommunicable attributes, we must always consider the full scope of what the Scriptures teach about God. Not only should we affirm divine transcendence, we must also acknowledge what the Bible reveals about God's immanence.

When we speak of divine immanence, we refer to the reality that God is involved with his creation. This is no small matter. The Bible devotes a great deal of time to revealing God's immanent involvement in the world, his manifestations of himself in the course of biblical history. In some cases, the Scriptures focus on God's historical manifestations in short periods of time. In other cases, they reflect on his historical displays over long periods of time. They deal with God's activities in his heavenly court and on earth. They disclose things about his interactions with the spiritual world and with the physical world, with large groups of people and with smaller groups, with families, and even with individuals.

Unfortunately, some well-meaning Christians have emphasized the Bible's attention to divine immanence to the point that they deny his transcendence. Some of these outlooks are more extreme than others, but in one way or another, they all stress divine immanence to such a degree that they reject God's incommunicable attributes.

For instance, it's become quite common to conclude that God must be finite in his knowledge because he asks questions. He is limited in power because he expresses frustration and doesn't carry out all his desires. Some theologians have suggested that God is not eternal because he waits to act until after he tests his people, he offers salvation, and he threatens judgment. These same theologians have concluded that the perfections of God are changeable because God answers prayer, relents, and revises the moral requirements he places on his people.

To deny that God is infinite, eternal, and unchangeable in these ways is also to strike at the heart of biblical faith. How can we be confident that God's purposes will not fail if God is limited in his power? How can we be sure that Christ has secured our eternal salvation if God is subject to time? How can we affirm that God's promises are reliable if God is changeable? As important as it is to affirm the immanence of God—his full engagement in history—we must also affirm what the Scriptures teach about the incommunicable attributes of God.

In the end, we must hold firmly to the full range of biblical perspectives on God's transcendence *and* his immanence. This isn't easy to do because we quickly reach the limits of our human understanding. As with many other difficult theological subjects, like the Trinity and the two natures of Christ, we come face to face with truths about God that are beyond our grasp. Yet, in the final analysis, the Scriptures call us to embrace both God's transcendence and his immanence, both the reality of God's incommunicable perfections *and* the reality of his engagement with his creation.

Psalm 115:3 succinctly summarizes this biblical point of view when it says, "Our God is in heaven; he does whatever pleases him." This verse views God's *transcendence* ("God is in heaven") as the basis for our confidence in his *immanence* ("he does whatever pleases him" in creation).

Theologians speak not only of the transcendence of God, how high and exalted he is, but also of the immanence of God, his closeness and the nearness of his presence. God is intimately involved in what is happening in the world, and he is very close to us. We see this supremely in Jesus Christ and in his incarnation, where the invisible Son of God became visible in the form of human flesh and actually came into our human situation. We also see the immanence of God in the nearness of the presence of God the Holy Spirit. This is one of the mysteries of the being and character of God. He is transcendent, far above us, but also immanent, near to us and close to us.

Philip Ryken

As mysterious as it is, God is infinite, but this doesn't mean that he's uninvolved with the finite. From the biblical point of view, it's precisely *because* God is infinite that he can fully enter the realm of the finite as he wishes. God is also eternal, but this doesn't mean that he's outside of time. Rather, his eternality is the reason that he can participate within time in any way he chooses. In addition, God is unchangeable, but this doesn't mean that he's not involved in our changing world. It's because God is unchangeable in all of his perfections that he engages his changing creation as he pleases. To gain a proper understanding of God's incommunicable attributes, we must embrace the full breadth of biblical teachings on God's transcendence and his immanence.

KEY TERMS AND CONCEPTS

divine immanence
divine transcendence
eternal
infinite
unchangeable

REVIEW QUESTIONS

1. How are God's incommunicable attributes grounded in the biblical doctrine of God's transcendence?
2. How can we say that even though the Augsburg Confession, Belgic Confession, and Westminster Shorter Catechism use different terminology to describe God's incommunicable attributes, they conceptually agree with each other?
3. How do the terms *infinite*, *eternal*, and *unchangeable* summarize what the Bible says about God's transcendence?
4. How does the doctrine of God's immanence help us to avoid misapplying God's transcendence?

DISCUSSION QUESTIONS

1. Why is it important to affirm that some of God's attributes are incommunicable to us?
2. What value do historic creeds and confessions hold for us today?
3. How can it comfort us that God isn't restricted by the limitations established for his creation?
4. Why does God need to investigate circumstances if he is omniscient?
5. Why does the Bible sometimes say that God changes his mind if he's immutable?

FOR FURTHER STUDY

Charnock, Stephen. *The Existence and Attributes of God*. Reprint, Grand Rapids: Baker Books, 2000.

Helm, Paul. *Eternal God: A Study of God without Time*. Oxford: Clarendon, 1988.

Packer, J. I. *Knowing God*. London: Hodder and Stoughton, 1973.

Reymond, Robert L. *A New Systematic Theology of the Christian Faith*. Nashville: Thomas Nelson, 1998.

CHAPTER QUIZ

https://thirdmill.org/quiz?GOD5

6

INTEGRATION OF
GOD'S ATTRIBUTES

It's been customary for systematic theologians to distinguish God's incommunicable and communicable attributes from each other. This has proven to be a useful distinction in many different ways. Yet biblical authors treated both classes of divine attributes as closely interconnected.

DIVINE SIMPLICITY

The integration of God's attributes accords with the longstanding Christian doctrine of the "simplicity of God." When theologians say that God is "simple," they don't mean that he's easy to understand. Rather, they have in mind that God's essence is not a composite; it's not divided. As the first article of the Augsburg Confession puts it, God is "without parts," and as the first article of the Belgic Confession expresses it, God is "one . . . simple and spiritual Being."

During the patristic and medieval periods, the influence of Hellenistic philosophies on leading Christian theologians made it easy to affirm the doctrine of God's simplicity. Hellenistic outlooks on God emphasized the absolute unity or oneness of God, and this backdrop led biblical interpreters to be keenly aware of this theme in the Scriptures. In more recent history, as the influence of Hellenistic philosophy has waned, a number of theologians have doubted that the Scriptures teach the simplicity or unity of God's essence. For this reason, it's important to point out the biblical foundation for this doctrine.

The doctrine of simplicity has been disputed over the centuries. What it does *not* mean is that God has no personality, no movement, no dynamism, no characteristics. It doesn't mean that he is simple in the sense that he is a platonic being with no attributes. Rather, it means that he's one kind of being. He does not add anything outside himself to himself. He's not composed of a bunch of parts added together, as some theologians think. God is a spirit. A spirit by definition is a simple being, not composed, not complex, not polytheistic.

This is ultimately a very comforting doctrine to us because it means our God is pure. He is not an amalgam of things that were put into his being or that he composed. It's not that he is simplistic or has no interest or intrigue or personality or love or attributes. It is that his being is not an addition of various parts. He is pure Spirit. **William Edgar**

Moses's well-known words "Hear, O Israel: The LORD our God, the LORD is one" (Deut. 6:4) have often been used to support belief in God's simplicity. This traditional translation implies the oneness or unity of God himself. Other English translators have offered other interpretations, including "The LORD our God is one LORD" (KJV); "The LORD is our God, the LORD is one" (NASB); or "The LORD is our God, the LORD alone" (NRSV). These modern alternatives suggest that this passage merely calls for Israel to serve Yahweh rather than other gods. Although the Hebrew grammar supports both of these possibilities, there is good reason to think that the traditional translation is superior.

In the book of Deuteronomy, Moses called Israel to be loyal to God and to turn away from all other gods. We know that, at times, the Israelites were tempted to total apostasy by utterly rejecting the Lord and serving the gods of other nations. More often, however, the Israelites fell into syncretism and mixed the beliefs and practices of other nations and religions with their own. These other nations referred to their gods, like Baal, Ashtaroth, and other gods, in the plural because they believed that these gods were divided, as it were, among different places. They acknowledged these gods one way in one place and another way in another place.

By contrast, Moses repeatedly taught Israel that they were to worship God at the one place that God ordained. Unlike the gods of other nations, God could not be divided into parts between one place and another because "the LORD is one." In this sense, Deuteronomy 6:4 lays a foundation for the Christian doctrine of the simplicity of God, the fact that God is not divided into parts.

James confirmed this understanding of Deuteronomy 6:4 when he wrote, "You believe that God is one; you do well" (James 2:19 ESV). James did not write, "You believe that *there is one God*," as some translations interpret it. He literally wrote, "You believe that God is one." In this way, James confirmed that Deuteronomy 6:4 teaches the oneness, the unity, the simplicity of God. God's perfections are not different parts of God. They are all fully unified, interconnected qualities of his one essence.

THEOLOGICAL VARIETY

As we saw earlier, even though theologians have used a variety of terms to sum up the incommunicable attributes of God, they have largely agreed on the concepts that their various terms signify. In many ways, the same is true of the integration of God's incommunicable attributes with his communicable attributes.

This integration has been expressed in a number of ways, yet to one degree or another, evangelical theologians have consistently affirmed the importance of integrating these two classes of attributes. To explore how this is true, let's look once again at the summaries of the attributes of God in the Augsburg Confession, the Belgic Confession, and the Westminster Shorter Catechism.

Augsburg Confession

You'll recall that the first article of the Augsburg Confession refers to God as "eternal, without body, without parts, of infinite power, wisdom, and goodness." As we mentioned earlier, the terms *eternal*, *without body*, *without parts*, and *infinite* are frequently associated with God's incommunicable attributes because he is different from his creation in these ways. The last three terms—*power, wisdom,* and *goodness*—are usually identified as communicable attributes because we can share these qualities with God on a creaturely scale. However, notice that the Confession doesn't treat these categories as entirely separate. It doesn't simply speak of God's power, wisdom and goodness. Rather, it adds the adjective *infinite* (or *immensus* in Latin). The grammar of the Latin text indicates that God is infinite in his power, infinite in his wisdom, and infinite in his goodness. In effect, the Augsburg Confession looks *through* God's infinity, through the fact that he is unlimited, and views his power, wisdom, and goodness in the light of his infinity, and in so doing, the Confession acknowledges that God's incommunicable attribute of infinity should be fully integrated with his communicable attributes.

Belgic Confession

The Belgic Confession, in turn, says that God is "eternal, incomprehensible, invisible, immutable, infinite, almighty, perfectly wise, just, [and] good."[1] We mentioned earlier that, more often than not, God's eternality, incomprehensibility, invisibility, immutability, and infinity are classified as incommunicable attributes. God's might, wisdom, justice, and goodness are most commonly identified as his communicable attributes. However, notice that the last four attributes are not listed simply as "mighty, wise, just, and good." Although

1. Belgic Confession, article 1.

our standard English translations don't make this clear, the original French here uses the phrases *tout puissant*, meaning "completely or perfectly mighty," and *tout sage*, meaning "completely or perfectly wise." In addition, the adjective *tout* can be extended implicitly to "just" and "good," so that we translate them *"perfectly* just" and *"perfectly* good." In other words, the Belgic Confession looks through the fact that God is infinite and views his might, wisdom, justice, and goodness in the light of his infinity. Although the Belgic Confession doesn't use exactly the same words as the Augsburg Confession, we can see that they both acknowledge the integrality of God's incommunicable and communicable attributes.

Westminster Shorter Catechism

In a similar way, you'll also recall that the answer to question 4 of the Westminster Shorter Catechism begins with the statement "God is a Spirit." It then lists three incommunicable attributes of God as Spirit: "infinite, eternal, and unchangeable." Still, rather than allowing us to think of these incommunicable perfections in isolation, the Shorter Catechism explains that all three of these incommunicable attributes are perfections of God "in his being, wisdom, power, holiness, justice, goodness, and truth."[2]

The Westminster Shorter Catechism's strategy for integrating God's attributes offers many advantages. To begin with, it uses three broad categories to summarize God's incommunicable attributes. How is God different from his creation? He is "infinite, eternal, and unchangeable." Then the Shorter Catechism answers the question of how God is infinite, eternal, and unchangeable. God is infinite "in his being, wisdom, power, holiness, justice, goodness, and truth." God is eternal "in his being, wisdom, power, holiness, justice, goodness, and truth." God is unchangeable "in his being, wisdom, power, holiness, justice, goodness, and truth." In effect, the Shorter Catechism provides a systematic way of exploring the full integration of God's incommunicable attributes with his communicable perfections.

---

2. Westminster Shorter Catechism, answer 4.

BIBLICAL PERSPECTIVES

As we have seen in this chapter, Scripture teaches that God is different from his creation in all, not just some, of his attributes. When we consider the full range of what the Bible teaches, it becomes increasingly clear that, in many ways, all of God's attributes are incommunicable.

We'll illustrate what we have in mind by following the strategy of the fourth question and answer in the Westminster Shorter Catechism. As we just saw, the Shorter Catechism claims that God is infinite, eternal, and unchangeable in each of the communicable attributes it identifies. To see how this outlook reflects the Scriptures, we'll take a look at all seven communicable attributes listed in the Catechism.

Being

In many respects, God's being or existence is an attribute that is communicable, or shared with God's creation. We know that everything that God has created, including human beings, actually exists, but we fail to grasp the glory of God's existence if we don't acknowledge a fundamental difference between God's being and our own. Our being is finite, temporal, and changeable, but God's being is infinite, eternal, and unchangeable. In traditional systematic theology this difference has often been highlighted by referring to God's immensity and omnipresence.

The immensity of God is his infinite, eternal, and unchangeable existence beyond creation. When Solomon dedicated the temple, he affirmed a grand theological presupposition that underlies everything in Scripture. He said, "The highest heaven, cannot contain [God]" (1 Kings 8:27). God is different from his creation in that his existence is in no way limited to the realm of his creation. He existed before there was a creation, he exists without limits currently, and he will continue to exist beyond all of creation forever.

The omnipresence of God can be defined as his existence everywhere within creation. Systematic theologians often point out that unlike any facet of the finite, time-bound, changeable creation, God is fully present in all places. As God himself put it, "Do not I fill heaven and earth?" (Jer. 23:24). Belief in the omnipresence of God is so basic to the biblical concept of God that Paul agreed with Greek poets who said that, "In [God] we live and move and have our being" (Acts 17:28; see also Ps. 139:7–10; Isa. 66:1; Acts 7:48–49).

One classic passage on which the doctrine of God's omnipresence is built is Acts 17:24–28, in which Paul, speaking at Athens, is amazed that God is able to reach even these pagan Gentiles. To explain this, he says that God is not just the God of the Jews but the God of all people everywhere, earth-wide, universe-wide, cosmic-wide. Along the way, Paul says that God is never far from any one of us, pagan or believer—in fact, he's the God in whom "we live and move and have our being." That is, he's everywhere.

To this passage we can add Jeremiah 23:23–24, which makes the point that we can't get away from God. We can run, but we can't hide, because God fills the whole earth. **R. Todd Mangum**

Wisdom

In many respects, wisdom is a communicable attribute of God shared by God's rational creatures. Even so, Scripture and general revelation make it clear that our wisdom is limited, temporal, and changeable. God is different from his creation in this respect because his wisdom is infinite, eternal, and unchangeable. Traditional systematic theologians typically stress the incommunicable dimensions of God's wisdom by referring to God's omniscience and his incomprehensibility.

The omniscience of God is the fact that God possesses knowledge of all things, including himself. Job 37:16 refers to God's perfect knowledge. Hebrews 4:13 says that "nothing in all creation is hidden from God's sight." Psalm 33:15 says that "[God] considers"—or understands—"everything [people] do." And in Jeremiah 23:24, God asked, "Can anyone hide in secret places so that I cannot see him?"

The incommunicable character of God's wisdom is also emphasized in the doctrine of the incomprehensibility of God. This terminology doesn't imply that we can't know anything of the mind of God. On the contrary, we know his thoughts as he reveals them to us. However, God's wisdom is incommunicable in the sense that God's thoughts cannot be fully known. As Paul said, God's judgments and paths are "unsearchable . . . beyond tracing out" (Rom. 11:33). Job 11:7 declares that we cannot "fathom the mysteries of God." In Psalm 139:6 the psalmist admitted that "[God's] knowledge is too wonderful . . . to attain." Similar passages also indicate that one of the ways God is different from his creation is that, unlike our human wisdom, God's wisdom is infinite, eternal, and unchangeable (e.g., 1 Sam. 16:7; 1 Chr. 28:9; Ps. 139:1–4; Jer. 17:10).

The wisdom of God is the transcendent thoughts that belong to God, that reside with him, and that he wants to share with us. The truth is, he wants us to live a life according to his transcendent, divine wisdom. But it's beyond us. Only by God's grace do we have an opportunity to attain to that level of living. We need the transcendent thoughts of God, and then, of course, his Holy Spirit to come live in us, so that we can not only live wisely but also think wisely and then articulate to others, "This is the way of wisdom."
Matt Friedeman

Power

Both the Scriptures and general revelation indicate many respects in which God's power is communicable to his creation, but even the greatest powers in creation are limited, temporal, and changeable. By contrast, God's power is infinite, eternal, and unchangeable. In systematic theology this contrast is most often expressed in terms of God's omnipotence and sovereignty.

When we speak of the omnipotence of God, we mean that God is all-powerful. For example, Job exclaimed, "You can do all things" (Job 42:2). Psalm 115:3 says that "[God] does whatever pleases him."

Jeremiah 32:17 praises God by saying, "Nothing is too hard for you," and Jesus reassured his disciples that "with God all things are possible" (Matt. 19:26).

We must be sure to add one important qualification here: God's power is always true to his other attributes. He can't do things that are contrary to the other perfections of his essence. For instance, God cannot lie, sin, change, nor deny himself (Num. 23:19; 1 Sam. 15:29; 2 Tim. 2:13; Heb. 6:18; James 1:13, 17). If we keep this qualification in mind, we can be assured that God is omnipotent in the sense that his power is infinite, eternal, and unchangeable.

Passages in the Bible that indicate that there are some things that God cannot do are not talking about the real meaning of God's omnipotence. He can only do that which is consistent with his nature. It would be totally inconsistent with his divine nature to lie, for example, so there are some things that God cannot do, but these things are totally within the realm of his nature. **Clete Hux**

Systematic theologians also refer to the sovereignty of God. Simply put, God's sovereignty is his absolute control over creation. Different branches of the church have disagreed over precisely how God exercises his sovereign control over creation, but the Scriptures teach that God has infinite, eternal, and unchangeable power to control everything. As King Jehoshaphat declared, "Power and might are in your hand, and no one can withstand you" (2 Chr. 20:6). Or as Job put it, "No plan of yours can be thwarted" (Job 42:2). Even King Nebuchadnezzar admitted that God "does as he pleases with the powers of heaven and the peoples of the earth" (Dan. 4:35). God's sovereignty is so extensive that he "works out everything in conformity with the purpose of his will" (Eph. 1:11). In addition, Paul assured us of God's sovereignty even during times of great trials because "in all things God works for the good of those who love him" (Rom. 8:28). These and countless other passages indicate that God's sovereignty is infinite, eternal, and unchangeable.

Holiness

God's holiness is one of his communicable attributes because it's shared by some facets of creation. The Scriptures frequently speak of locations, objects, spirits, and people as holy. The biblical adjectives that we usually translate as "holy," "sacred," or "sanctified"— *qādôš* in Hebrew and *hagios* in Greek—simply mean "separate" or "set apart." Still, both general revelation and the Scriptures disclose that the holiness of creatures is finite, temporal, and changeable, while God's holiness is not. In systematics, theologians most often approach the incommunicable qualities of God's holiness by calling attention to his moral holiness and to his majestic holiness.

The moral holiness of God is his separation from all evil. As Psalm 92:15 puts it, "there is no wickedness in him." Similarly, Habakkuk 1:12–13 exclaims, "Holy One. . . . Your eyes are too pure to look on evil; you cannot tolerate wrong." God's moral purity is so basic to biblical faith that James wrote, "God cannot be tempted with evil, and he himself tempts no one" (James 1:13 ESV).

The Scriptures also point to God's majestic holiness. This terminology indicates that God is separate from all creation, including his morally pure creatures. God's majestic holiness is most vividly illustrated in Isaiah 6:3 where seraphim cry out, "Holy, holy, holy is the LORD Almighty." Seraphim are morally pure creatures who serve before the throne of God, but in this passage, they acknowledge that God is to be worshipped as utterly supreme in his holiness (see also Ex. 15:11; 1 Sam. 2:2; Isa. 57:15; Hos. 11:9).

The difference between God's moral holiness and his ontological, or majestic, holiness goes back to the idea of what the word *holy* means. It essentially means "set apart from." God is set apart in two ways. First, he is set apart from sinners. He is pure; he never sins; he is perfectly righteous; and so he's set apart from sinners in that regard—as one who is morally perfect and pure. Second, God is set apart because he is higher than us; he is different from us; he is of a different nature and ontological status—a higher being—

and in that respect is holy as well. His ways and his thoughts are far above ours. He is holy—that is, set apart—both in his being and in the righteousness of his character. **Dan Hendley**

Justice

Both general and special revelation indicate that justice is a communicable attribute because moral creatures, especially human beings, can be just and righteous. The concept of God's justice is often expressed by the family of Hebrew terms associated with the word ṣaddîq, and with the family of Greek terms associated with the term dikaiosynē. We normally translate these terms as "righteousness" or "justice," but while human righteousness and justice are limited, temporal, and changing, God's righteousness or justice is infinite, eternal, and unchangeable.

In Scripture, the attribute of God's justice is most often associated with the judgments of his heavenly court. As Peter wrote, we have a Father who "judges each man's work impartially" (1 Peter 1:17). According to Paul, in "righteous judgment . . . God 'will give to each person according to what he has done'" (Rom. 2:5–6). Because God's judgments are always true, Paul went on to ask, "Is God unjust?" And his reply was firm: "Not at all!" (Rom. 9:14). Moses also declared, "All his ways are just. . . . Upright and just is he" (Deut. 32:4). So, it's no wonder that Jesus called his heavenly Father "Righteous" (or just) "Father" (John 17:25). In light of this association between divine justice and the heavenly court, systematic theologians have drawn attention to God's justice in two main areas: his just rewards and the just punishments he dispenses.

God's nature is to grant just rewards for righteousness. As Psalm 58:11 puts it, "The righteous still are rewarded [because] . . . there is a God who judges the earth." Paul referred to the righteousness that comes to all who are justified in Christ when he spoke of "the crown of righteousness, which the Lord, the righteous Judge, will award . . . to all who have longed for his appearing" (2 Tim. 4:8). It may seem at times as if there is no reward for righteousness, but we can be assured of God's just rewards because God remains infinite, eternal, and unchangeable in his justice.

It's also God's nature to grant just punishments for evil. Paul insisted that "God is just. . . . He will punish those who do not know God and do not obey the gospel of our Lord Jesus" (2 Thess. 1:6–8). Paul also called for repentance because "[God] has set a day when he will judge the world with justice by the man he has appointed" (Acts 17:31). In fact, the just punishment of God against sin is a pillar of biblical faith. As Paul explained, God is both "just and the one who justifies" (Rom. 3:26) because Christ's atonement met the requirement of justice on behalf of all who believe. These and many other passages draw attention to how God's infinite, eternal, and unchangeable justice is displayed in his just punishments.

Goodness

We should begin by emphasizing that there is no measure of goodness outside God that God must meet. God himself is the very definition of good. As the first article of the Belgic Confession puts it, God is "good, and the overflowing fountain of all good." That being said, goodness is clearly a communicable attribute because the Scriptures often refer to creation as good. God himself called creation "very good" (Gen. 1:31), and Paul reaffirmed this divine declaration (1 Tim. 4:4).

In Scripture, "good" is often translated from the words *ṭôb* in Hebrew and *agathos* in Greek. Both words signify the approval of someone or something. When God approves of something in creation, that something is "good" in a limited, temporal, and changeable way. However, when the Scriptures say that God is "good," they mean that he is infinitely, eternally, and unchangeably deserving of approval. In systematic theology, God's goodness is closely associated with a number of familiar biblical teachings, but it helps to think in terms of two main categories: the *direct goodness* of God and the *indirect goodness* of God.

When we speak of the direct goodness of God, we have in mind

God's goodness shown in things like his benevolence, mercy, love, and patience toward his creatures. For instance, Psalm 34:8 speaks of God's benevolence as the proof of his goodness when it says, "Taste and see that the LORD is good." God's goodness is associated with his mercy and compassion in Exodus 33:19, where God said to Moses, "I will cause all my goodness to pass in front of you. . . . I will have mercy on whom I will have mercy, and I will have compassion on whom I will have compassion." Psalm 25:7 speaks of God's love flowing from his goodness when it says, "According to your love remember me, for you are good, O LORD."

Scripture points to God's direct goodness in many different ways (see, for example, Pss. 23:6; 73:1; 145:9, 15–16; Mark 10:18), but the most direct display of the infinite, eternal, and unchangeable goodness of God is his eternal love for Christ and for all those who are in Christ. As Paul put it: "In love he predestined us to be adopted as his sons through Jesus Christ, in accordance with his pleasure and will—to the praise of his glorious grace, which he has freely given us in the One he loves" (Eph. 1:4–6). As the larger context of this verse makes clear, our adoption to sonship was in love—the love of God for us from before the creation, and God's eternal love for his people is in Christ, who is "the One he loves." The love of God for those who are in Christ is rooted in the infinite, eternal, and unchanging love of the Father for his Son.

The Bible tells us much about God's love for us. God loves us in many ways, and he shows us his love for us in many ways. However, the Bible is clear that God definitively and ultimately shows his love for us by sending his only Son to us. John 3:16 says, "God so loved the world that he gave his one and only Son." God's love is most supremely demonstrated, then, in the giving of his Son to the world in order to save the world.

But we must not stop there. God's love is demonstrated in what he gave his Son to do for us. His Son came to be a sacrifice for our sins. We are not the ones who loved God, but God loved us and sent his Son to be a propitiation

for our sins, and this should bring great encouragement to us. Paul picks up on this point and encourages us with these words: "[If God] did not spare his own Son, but gave him up for us all—how will he not also . . . with him [freely] give us all things?" (Rom. 8:32). God has definitively and ultimately and climactically shown us the way he loves us in the giving of his Son. We should, therefore, trust him and be assured that he really does love us.
Brandon D. Crowe

Scripture also draws attention to God's goodness by focusing on God's indirect goodness. Here we have in mind the assurance that God will bring about good even through troubles and trials that temporarily plague his creation. One of the greatest challenges to belief in God's goodness is the presence of evil in his creation, but biblical authors insisted that the perfection of God's goodness will cause good to result from evil. For example, James wrote that difficult trials are for our good (James 1:2–4) and that "every good and perfect gift is from above, coming down from the Father of the heavenly lights" (James 1:17). Similarly, Paul assured the Roman Christians that "we know that in all things God works for the good of those who love him" (Rom. 8:28).

Truth

Both the Bible and general revelation make it clear that God's attribute of truth is also a communicable attribute. God's rational and moral creatures can be true, honest, reliable, and faithful. The concept of God's truth is expressed in the family of Hebrew terms associated with the verb 'āman (often translated "to be sure," "confirmed," or "true") and from the well-known term ḥesed (often translated "faithfulness" or "lovingkindness"). It's also expressed in the New Testament Greek terms associated with alētheia and pistis. These biblical terms signify veracity, truthfulness, reliability, and faithfulness. God's creatures can exhibit these qualities, but only in finite, temporal, and changing ways. By contrast, the truth of God is infinite, eternal, and unchangeable. Paul reflected on this contrast when he wrote, "Let God be true, and every man a liar" (Rom. 3:4). By and large, systematic theologians have highlighted this divine attribute by noting that God is the source of all truth and that he is faithful to his promises.

Scripture frequently extols God as the faithful source of truth. The psalmist spoke of the Scriptures as God's "word of truth" (Ps. 119:43) and confidently declared, "Your law is true" (Ps. 119:142). Psalm 25:5 reads, "Guide me in your truth and teach me." In the New Testament, Jesus explained to his disciples that if they held to his teaching, they would "know the truth, and the truth [would] set [them] free" (John 8:32). He also promised his apostles that "the Spirit of truth" would guide them "into all truth" (John 16:13), and in his high priestly prayer, Jesus prayed to the Father, "Sanctify them by the truth; your word is truth" (John 17:17). In these and other ways, the Scriptures teach that every revelation of God is fully reliable because it is his very nature to be faithful and true.

God is also infinitely, eternally, and unchangeably truthful and faithful to his promises. God can be relied upon to fulfill all his promises. Now, we have to be careful here. Many times in Scripture what may *appear* to be a promise from God is actually an offer or a threat from God with implicit conditions (2 Sam. 12:13–22; Jer. 18:7–10; Jonah 3:4–10). If the implicit conditions aren't met, God's offer or threat is not fulfilled, but "God . . . does not lie" (Titus 1:2). If God makes a promise, he will fulfill it (Num. 23:19; Ps. 33:4; Heb. 6:18). He faithfully fulfills all his promises. It's no surprise, then, that Revelation 3:14 introduces the exalted Christ as, "the faithful and true witness, the ruler of God's creation."

We've only touched on a few of the many things that could be said about this facet of the doctrine of God, but the Westminster Shorter Catechism gives us glimpses into the breadth of biblical perspectives we must consider as we learn about God's incommunicable perfections. As we've seen, the Scriptures don't present him as infinite, eternal, and unchangeable in just *some* ways, but in *every* way. Every facet of God's essence is beyond compare, and in this sense, *every* attribute of God is incommunicable.

Our beliefs about the ways God is different from his creation are so vital to the Christian faith that they impact all our doctrines, practices, and attitudes. Many pillars of Christian doctrine rest on a proper understanding of God's incommunicable perfections. Our daily activities are guided by these truths as well, and our attitudes of humility, confidence, joy, and worship before God are deeply influenced by what we believe about this facet of theology proper. Understanding what the Scriptures teach about the incommunicable attributes of God equips us for every dimension of faithful service in Christ.

KEY TERMS AND CONCEPTS

being
divine simplicity
goodness
holiness
justice
power
truth
wisdom

REVIEW QUESTIONS

1. What is divine simplicity?
2. Why is it important to integrate God's incommunicable and communicable attributes?
3. How is God's wisdom different from ours? How can God's attribute of wisdom be communicated to us?
4. In what sense might we say that all God's attributes are incommunicable?

DISCUSSION QUESTIONS

1. What does the attribute of God's wisdom teach us about how God is different from us and how we can become more like him?

2. What do we mean when we say that God's power must be true to or consistent with his attributes?
3. How is understanding God's "majestic holiness" important for our Christian life?
4. How should we distinguish God's justice from his goodness?
5. How does the truth of God give us confidence that we can trust him?

FOR FURTHER STUDY

Bavinck, Herman. *Reformed Dogmatics*. Edited by John Bolt. Translated by John Vriend. 4 vols. Grand Rapids: Baker Academic, 2003–8.

Berkhof, Louis. *Systematic Theology*. New ed. Grand Rapids: Eerdmans, 1996.

Grudem, Wayne. *Systematic Theology: An Introduction to Biblical Doctrine*. Grand Rapids: Zondervan, 1994.

Helm, Paul. *Eternal God: A Study of God without Time*. Oxford: Clarendon, 1988.

Lewis, C. S. *A Grief Observed*. 1961. Reprint, New York: HarperOne, 2001.

———. *The Problem of Pain*. 1940. Reprint, New York: HarperOne, 2001.

Reymond, Robert L. *A New Systematic Theology of the Christian Faith*. Nashville: Thomas Nelson, 1998.

CHAPTER QUIZ

https://thirdmill.org/quiz?GOD6

PART TEST

https://thirdmill.org/quiz?GOD2s

PART 3

HOW GOD IS LIKE US

A story is told of a highly respected mathematics scholar and teacher. His books and lectures went far beyond the reach of the average person and often beyond the reach of his most advanced students, but one day, the reputation of this world-famous professor changed forever. Several international students spent Christmas Day with him and his family, and they saw a side of him they had never imagined. Surrounded by his grandchildren and guests, this erudite professor sat on the floor, happily playing games designed for four- and five-year-olds. The students reported the next day, "It was hard to believe that someone like him could be so much like us."

In many respects, the Scriptures teach this same kind of thing about God. They make it clear that God transcends his creation—he is utterly different—but they also reveal many similarities between God and creation. As hard as it may be to understand, the Scriptures teach that God is also like us.

7

GOD'S COMMUNICABLE
ATTRIBUTES IN SCRIPTURE

Earlier, we defined God's attributes as the perfections of God's essence revealed through a variety of historical manifestations. In this section, we'll turn our attention to the communicable attributes of God. Because of our human limitations, we face countless mysteries as we explore what the Scriptures teach about God. This is certainly true when we deal with God's communicable attributes.

We've seen that God is utterly different from his creation—not just in some of his perfections, but in *all* of them—but at the same time, everyone familiar with the Bible knows that it often describes God and his creation as if they were similar. Words like *holy, just, righteous, good, faithful, loving,* and *powerful* are applied both to God and to various aspects of creation. So, as difficult as it may be for us to fathom how these two perspectives fit together, biblical faith calls on us to affirm that God is both different from and similar to his creation.

BIBLICAL COMPARISONS BETWEEN
GOD AND CREATION

Previously, we mentioned that medieval Scholastic theologians focused a great deal on natural theology. They sought to learn about God by observing nature without much direct attention to the Scriptures, and they identified three formal strategies for discerning truths about God from nature: "the way of negation" (or *via negationis*), "the way of causation" (or *via causalitatis*), and "the way of eminence" (or *via eminentiae*).

Throughout the centuries, Protestant theologians have rightly agreed that we can learn a lot about God from nature in these ways, but Protestants have also emphasized that we need the guidance of special revelation in Scripture. Scripture serves, as it were, like eyeglasses that bring clarity to what God has disclosed about himself in general revelation. John Calvin wrote in his *Institutes of the Christian Religion*, "Just as . . . those with weak vision . . . with the aid of spectacles will begin to read distinctly; so Scripture, gathering up the otherwise confused knowledge of God in our minds, having dispersed our dullness, clearly shows us the true God."[1] To unpack this a bit, we'll consider how Scripture itself uses the three basic strategies we've mentioned—the ways of negation, causation, and eminence.

Natural theology is what we can learn from nature. Special revelation refers to how God reveals himself not in nature—in our own persons, in the world around us—but in Scripture and ultimately in Christ through his Holy Spirit. Romans 1 and Psalm 8 tell us that God's invisible qualities have been shown in the world around us in creation. For those who have eyes to see, this is clear. The trouble is that we don't have eyes to see—we're blind—so God has revealed himself in a special way, in a particular way, ultimately in Christ at the cross, as witnessed by his Word, the Old and New Testaments.
Josh Moody

General revelation always exists—we see it in things like the sky, the moral law, and conscience at work in people. In the end, however, the only thing general revelation gives us is a knowledge that God exists, that God is

1. John T. McNeill, ed., *Calvin: Institutes of the Christian Religion*, trans. Ford Lewis Battles (Philadelphia: Westminster Press, 1960), 1.6.1.

powerful, and that God is eternal. Only through special revelation can we understand this eternally existing, powerful God to be holy, righteous, good, loving, and merciful. Understanding special revelation is like finding the master key and then using this key to decode general revelation; everything becomes visible and clear after that. **Stephen Tong (translation)**

Way of Negation

In brief, the way of negation amounts to inferring truths about God by contrasting him with creation. Biblical authors repeatedly drew attention to contrasts between God and his creation—not simply contrasts with sin and evil (Num. 23:19; James 1:20; 1 John 1:5), but also with the good qualities that God gave his creation (1 Cor. 1:19–25; 1 John 3:20)—and they frequently honored God by pointing out that he transcends all comparisons. For this reason, this approach primarily draws our attention toward God's incommunicable attributes, but in doing so, it sets the stage for our focus on the communicable attributes of God. Ultimately, we can't begin to see how God is like us without first realizing how entirely different from us he is. So, in order to understand God's communicable attributes rightly, Scripture's use of the way of negation reminds us of the great mystery that, in one way or another, all God's attributes are incommunicable.

Way of Causation

Unlike the way of negation, the way of causation primarily points us toward God's communicable attributes. In Scripture, the way of causation opens a path for discerning how God is like us by comparing God with the good things he's made (Ps. 8:3–4; Rom. 1:20). Common experience teaches us that a painting reflects the skills, emotions, and thoughts of its artist, and a piece of music reflects the talents and imagination of its composer. As a result, we can learn a lot about artists and composers by studying what they've made. In many ways, biblical authors did much the same when they drew conclusions about God from their observations of what God had made. Knowing that God is the First Cause, or Creator, they inferred what must be true about him by noting the good qualities he bestowed on his creation.

The Scriptures make use of the way of causation in two primary ways. For one, they offer direct comparisons between God and what he has made. For instance, Psalm 94:9 employs this strategy: "Does he who implanted the ear not hear? Does he who formed the eye not see?" The psalmist believed that because God made our ears and eyes, we can be confident that God himself has the ability to hear and see.

What kind of God creates the beauty of the earth, except God who is himself beautiful? What kind of God creates order, except God who is himself orderly? What kind of God can give life, except the living God? There is no end to the truths we can learn about God by noting the good things God has made.

In addition to direct comparisons, biblical authors also employed the way of causation when they made figurative comparisons between God and his creation. At times, these comparisons involved inanimate objects. For instance, Isaiah wrote, "The Light of Israel will become a fire, their Holy One a flame; in a single day it will burn and consume" (Isa. 10:17). As the larger context of this passage indicates, God was going to destroy the empire of Assyria. To explain how this would happen, Isaiah referred to God metaphorically as a "fire" and a "flame" that would "burn and consume." In effect, Isaiah drew upon the similarities between the consuming powers of fire and the consuming power of God.

The same kind of reasoning lies behind other metaphors for God, like those in Psalm 18:2 where the psalmist said, "The LORD is my rock, my fortress . . . my God is my rock, in whom I take refuge. He is my shield and the horn of my salvation, my stronghold." Here we see that the psalmist compared God to several things God had made: a great "rock" or boulder, a "fortress," a "shield," a "horn," and a "stronghold." He did this to express how God had protected him and had secured him against his foes.

The Scriptures also compare God to animals. For example, Moses said, "[God] shielded [Jacob] and cared for him . . . like an eagle that stirs up its nest and hovers over its young" (Deut. 32:10–11). Along these same lines, Psalm 91:4 tells us, "[God] will cover you with his feathers, and under his wings you will find refuge."

There are countless ways in which the Bible appeals to similarities between God and what he has made, and this prominent biblical outlook establishes a foundation for exploring the many ways God is like his creation.

> Figurative comparisons are essential if we are to understand God and his attributes. We cannot comprehend God. God is not just man on a larger scale. God is God, and so, as God condescends to us and reveals himself to us, he doesn't reveal himself to us in ways that we can't understand and can't comprehend. Rather, God demonstrates his grace and mercy by revealing himself to us in ways that are connected to the things that we can understand. These figurative representations, examples, analogies, metaphors, and similes are the only way that we can begin to put together the building blocks for understanding who God is. **Voddie Baucham Jr.**

Way of Eminence

The way of eminence points us to God's superiority or greatness. This approach also helps us to identify the communicable attributes of God by making comparisons between God and his creation, but this third strategy is based on the biblical outlook that, even when God is similar to his creation, he is always far superior, far greater than anything he has made (Matt. 7:11; Heb. 6:13; 1 John 5:9). As Paul put it, "God, the blessed and only Ruler, the King of kings and Lord of lords, who alone is immortal and who lives in unapproachable light, whom no one has seen or can see. To him be honor and might forever" (1 Tim. 6:15–16). By speaking of God as "Ruler," "King," and "Lord," Paul affirmed that God is similar to human rulers, kings, and lords, but notice also how Paul stressed the superiority of God over all others. He is the *"only* Ruler," the "King *of kings,"* and the "Lord *of lords."* Only God is immortal, and only he lives in unapproachable light.

Throughout the Scriptures, we find that God has endowed his creation with power, complexity, vastness, goodness, wonder, and the like. In these and many other ways, there are similarities between God and his creation. However, while this is the case, the Scriptures repeatedly show that God's power, complexity, vastness, goodness, and wonder are far greater, far beyond what exists in creation. In this sense, the way of eminence in Scripture helps us to remember that God is superior to us, even as he is like us.

As we can see, biblical authors followed all three traditional strategies for discerning truths about God—the way of negation, the way of causation, and the way of eminence. Taken together, these basic strategies establish firm biblical foundations for exploring how God is similar to his creation.

BIBLICAL OUTLOOKS ON HUMANITY

The Scriptures testify that creation in general is like God in many ways, and we can learn a lot about God by carefully studying his creation, but the Scriptures also teach that we can learn even more about God by reflecting on human beings. God has granted humanity, more than any other facet of creation, the honor of being like him, and this resemblance establishes a firm biblical basis for exploring the communicable perfections of God.

Modern science has made us more aware of the vast expanses of the universe, so it's easy to underestimate the significance of human beings. We are but tiny specks on our planet; our planet is little more than a blue dot in our solar system; our solar system is a miniscule portion of our galaxy; and there are countless, immense galaxies throughout the universe. For this reason, it may seem that human beings are far too insignificant to be considered when we want to learn about God, but as tiny as we are, the Scriptures teach that, in reality, human beings are the crown of God's creation. As we read in Psalm 8:3–5, "When I consider your heavens, the work of your fingers, the moon and the stars, which you have set in place, what is man that you are mindful of him, the son of man that you care for him? You made him a little lower than the heavenly beings and crowned him with glory and honor." Humanity may seem small and insignificant compared to the heavens, but despite appearances, God actually made us just a little lower than the angels and gave us glory and honor. In addition, as the author of Hebrews explained, even humanity's subordination to angels is only temporary (Heb. 2:5–9). When Christ returns in glory, human beings who have followed him will be exalted above the greatest spiritual creatures.

The Scriptures first acknowledge human beings' special status in Genesis 1:26, where God said, "Let us make man in our image, in our likeness." In distinction from every other creature, human beings are the image and likeness of God. Now, the full range of this biblical teaching about humanity goes far beyond the scope of this present volume. So, we'll simply note that the expressions *image* and *likeness* affirm that human beings resemble God more than any other facet of creation. God made human beings like himself so we could serve as his royal and priestly representatives by filling and subduing the earth for his glory.

In the beginning, our first parents were without blemish. Later on, sin and rebellion against God corrupted every facet of human existence, but passages like Genesis 9:6 and James 3:9 indicate that even sinful, rebellious human beings continue to be honored as the image and likeness of God. More than this, God calls and equips men and women whom Christ has redeemed to turn from their sin and be renewed in his likeness. As Paul wrote: "You were taught, with regard to your former way of life, to put off your old self, which is being corrupted by its deceitful desires; to be made new in the attitude of your minds; and to put on the new self, created to be like God in true righteousness and holiness" (Eph. 4:22–24).

Because human beings are the image and likeness of God, the Scriptures frequently reveal who God is by comparing him with human beings. To mention just a few examples, some passages refer to God as Father and compare him with human fathers (Matt. 7:11). Some passages compare God to a gardener (Isa. 5:1–7; John 15:1). In various places, God is described as a king (Num. 23:21; 1 Tim. 1:17), a shepherd (Gen. 48:15; Heb. 13:20), and a husband (Isa. 54:5). The list of comparisons could go on and on. Of course, the way of eminence reminds us that God is superior to any human father, gardener, king, shepherd, or husband. Still, these and countless other comparisons demonstrate that we can learn a lot about God through our understanding of human beings.

Can we have awareness of God and his attributes without gaining at least some awareness of ourselves in the process? The answer is that awareness of God and self-awareness always go together. John Calvin makes this point integral to his *Institutes of the Christian Religion*. At the beginning, there was knowledge of God and knowledge of self. Without the knowledge of God, there is no knowledge of self. We were made to be drawn to him, and so the knowledge of him draws us to a knowledge of ourselves, and a true knowledge of ourselves is integral to knowing him as well. **Richard Phillips**

Throughout the history of the church, Christian theologians have articulated a variety of ways in which human beings are like God, but by and large, they've concentrated on three main human characteristics. We'll spend more time on these traits in the next chapter, so for now we'll simply provide an overview of these three human characteristics.

Intellectual Character

Theologians have emphasized what the Scriptures teach about the intellectual character of human beings. Even though our fall into sin has corrupted our minds, we are still intellectually superior to other earthly creatures. To be sure, the mind of God is far greater than the human mind, but our creaturely intellectual abilities still make us similar to God. As the Bible tells us, in many ways, God thinks, plans, and reasons, much like we do.

Volitional Character

Theologians have often stressed the volitional character of human beings—the fact that God has endowed us with human will. Again, sin has corrupted the human will, but unlike a rock or some other inanimate object, God has endowed us with the ability to make choices. We know, of course, that God's will is far superior to the human will, but our ability to exercise our will still makes us like God.

Moral Character

Theologians have emphasized the moral character of human beings as another way we are like God. Unlike any other physical creature, our thoughts and choices have moral qualities. Now, God's moral character is utterly perfect and thus far above anything we could ever achieve. Still, along with angels and demons, human beings are held responsible for the moral qualities of the choices they make.

These three human characteristics have provided direction for systematic theologians to explore God's communicable attributes. What the Scriptures say about the intellectual, volitional, and moral qualities of human existence has held center stage in formal discussions of how God is like his creation.

KEY TERMS AND CONCEPTS

image of God
likeness of God
intellectual character
moral character
volitional character
way of causation

way of eminence
way of negation

REVIEW QUESTIONS

1. What can we learn about God through the "way of negation"?
2. What kinds of things can we learn about God through the creatures he has designed and the beauty of the natural world?
3. What special status do human beings have over God's creation? What does this teach us about our need to be like God?
4. How does Scripture call for us to be like God in our intellect, our will, and our moral character?

DISCUSSION QUESTIONS

1. What do you see as limitations to the three aspects of natural theology described in this chapter?
2. What do biblical metaphors for God teach us about God's relationship to the natural world?
3. Why is it so important for us to ascribe preeminence to God alone?
4. If we are created in God's image, why do we need God's grace in order to become more like him?
5. How has sin corrupted our ability to understand, obey, and worship God in our lives?

FOR FURTHER STUDY

Berkhof, Louis. *Systematic Theology*. New ed. Grand Rapids: Eerdmans, 1996.

Kaiser, Christopher B. *The Doctrine of God*. Westchester, IL: Good News, 1982.

Macleod, Donald. *Behold Your God*. 2nd ed. Fearn, UK: Christian Focus, 1995.

Tozer, A. W. *The Knowledge of the Holy.* New York: Harper and Row, 1961.

Wenham, John W. *The Goodness of God.* London: InterVarsity Press, 1974.

CHAPTER QUIZ

https://thirdmill.org/quiz?GOD7

8

GOD'S COMMUNICABLE
ATTRIBUTES IN THEOLOGY

It is one thing to recognize the various ways the Scriptures teach that God is like his creation, but as we're about to see, it's quite another thing to grasp how systematic theologians have built on these biblical foundations. Traditional Christian theologians have sought to determine as precisely as possible how God's perfections—his infinite, eternal, and unchangeable attributes—are communicable. To do this, they've asked a number of crucial questions. What are these attributes? How are they reflected in creation, especially in human beings? And what is the best way to formulate coherent outlooks on this facet of theology proper?

THEOLOGICAL PROCESSES

One of the greatest challenges facing systematic theologians is that biblical teachings on God's attributes are scattered throughout Scripture. The Bible never gives us a complete, authoritative list of God's attributes, and it never methodically defines or explains them. So, to fulfill their task, systematic theologians have had to discern these various shapes and colors, and synthesize them into composite portraits, or stained-glass windows, as it were. To create these syntheses, systematic theologians have employed a number of processes. For our purposes, we'll focus on two of the more prominent ones.

Technical Terms

The Scriptures use a wide range of vocabulary to signify God's communicable perfections. In fact, biblical authors often used different expressions to signify the same concepts. They also used the same terms in various passages to signify different concepts. Therefore, to create faithful syntheses of biblical teachings about God's attributes, theologians have adopted technical terms. In other words, they've chosen to use certain expressions and assigned these expressions special meanings.

Now, if every systematic theologian used the same technical terms in precisely the same ways, formal discussions of God's communicable attributes would be much simpler. Unfortunately, they don't. For instance, some theologians have spoken of God's "wisdom" as a broad category that includes God's knowledge. Others have sharply distinguished between God's wisdom and knowledge. In a similar way, some theologians have referred to the "goodness" of God as a broad category. They've included what the Scriptures teach about God's grace, mercy, love, and related terms, as expressions of his goodness. Other theologians, however, have defined God's goodness, grace, mercy, and love in very distinct ways.

Theologians have characterized, or organized, God's attributes in many different ways to better understand who God is. The simplest way to think about it is: What are things that human beings are meant to be like and are meant to do that God is like and that God does? **Vermon Pierre**

For these and similar reasons, it's always important not to worry too much about the particular words that systematic theologians choose to use. The goal of evangelical systematic theology is to create faithful summaries of the *concepts* of Scripture, not to mimic the diverse vocabulary of Scripture. Similarly, biblical concepts about God can be expressed in a variety of technical terms.

Theological Propositions

Theological propositions are the basic building blocks of every facet of systematic theology. Broadly speaking, a theological proposition is a sentence that asserts as directly as possible at least one factual theological claim. This straightforward approach to God's communicable attributes seems simple enough, but the Scriptures reveal God's communicable attributes in many different genres: narrative, poetry, law, prophecy, epistles, and so on. Each of these genres has different ways of expressing truths about God. To create logically coherent presentations of these biblical teachings, systematic theologians have had to infer theological propositions from every biblical genre.

The question of theological method focuses on Scripture because Scripture is the primary source and the absolute authority, or norm, for all our theology. Thus, when we go to Scripture, we're always trying to ask the theological question of Scripture: What is being taught to us here?

As we're driven into Scripture, we immediately find that Scripture is not a manual of systematic theology or anything like it. Scripture has an overarching narrative structure, and much of Scripture is narrative in a strict sense. We also have the Psalms, the parables, and many other genres in Scripture. And so we are faced with significant exegetical questions about how we move from understanding the text, as it has been given to us, to drawing the teaching out of the text in such a way that it can become useful for theological formulation and argument. There are statements in Scripture that are very, very direct about God, but a lot of the theology in Scripture requires working to conclusions about him based on what has been written. We have to employ certain basic exegetical principles in order to understand the text rightly on its own terms. When we have done so, we get insight into who God is. **Bruce Baugus**

This process of inferring theological propositions is easier with some biblical passages than with others. For instance, the Scriptures contain many claims that are already in the form of propositions about the perfections of God. David's poetic song in Psalm 34:8 tells us "the LORD is good." In 1 John 4:8, we read that "God is love." These kinds of biblical propositions fit easily into formal theological discussions about God's communicable attributes.

Other Scriptures offer what amount to rather straightforward descriptions of God. For example, in the prophetic words of Isaiah 1:4, we find that God is described as "the Holy One." It's not difficult to see how systematic theologians have transformed this description into the simple proposition: "God is holy." In the genre of law in Deuteronomy 7:9, God is described as "the faithful God." In other words, "God is faithful."

However, not all biblical passages fit so easily into formal systematic theology. When dealing with biblical narratives, we can often infer many different propositional statements from the same story. For instance, the account of creation in Genesis 2 illustrates that "God is powerful," "God is wise," and "God is good." The story of Sodom and Gomorrah in Genesis 19 illustrates that "God is holy," "God is merciful," and "God is just." Every biblical narrative has given systematic theologians opportunities to infer a variety of propositions about the communicable attributes of God.

We also see God's communicable attributes in places where the Bible relies heavily on figures of speech such as metaphors, similes, and analogies. This is especially apparent in biblical poetry. For example, poetic passages like Psalm 89:26 and prophetic passages like Isaiah 64:8 speak of God as "father"—a metaphor that tells us many different things about God. However, instead of using the multifaceted imagery of God as "father," systematic theologians have been more inclined to use straightforward propositions like "God is good." Poetic passages like Psalm 24:8 and Exodus 15:3 and narrative passages like Joshua 23:10 portray God as a warrior, but systematic theologians have typically narrowed their focus to a proposition like "God is powerful." And on the basis of poetic passages like Psalm 118:27 and 1 John 1:5, we could say that, "God is light." But systematic theologians have been more inclined to translate this metaphor into a proposition like "God is morally pure."

We can see that figures of comparison like these reveal that God is like his creation. Employing figurative language enriches our discussions of God's communicable attributes, but systematic theologians have been more focused on presenting these same truths about God in the form of straightforward theological propositions. By doing so, they've been able to create logically coherent teachings on the communicable attributes of God.

HISTORICAL DOCUMENTS

If we were to survey the works of leading evangelical theologians, it would quickly become evident that their views on God's communicable attributes are usually very similar. We could refer to any number of lists Christians have used throughout church history to express how God is like us, but for the sake of simplicity, we'll consider the three historical documents that we've already mentioned several times: the Augsburg Confession, the Belgic Confession, and the Westminster Shorter Catechism. These documents represent common ways evangelicals have developed formal summaries of God's communicable perfections.

Augsburg Confession

You'll recall that the first article of the Augsburg Confession summarizes God's attributes in this way: "There is one Divine Essence which is called and which is God: eternal, without body, without parts, of infinite power, wisdom, and goodness." This article first mentions elements that have commonly been identified as God's *incommunicable* attributes—how he is *different* from his creation—but the Confession also mentions God's power, wisdom, and goodness. These three attributes are commonly identified as communicable attributes, or ways in which God is like his creation, especially like human beings.

God has endowed creation with each of these perfections, but on a smaller scale. Passages like Psalm 68:34–35 teach that God possesses power and that he has endowed his creation with a similar, although lesser, power. Passages like Daniel 2:20–21 reveal that God possesses wisdom and that he has granted a degree of wisdom to human beings. Passages like Psalm 119:68 and 2 Peter 1:3–5 indicate not only that God is good but also that he has placed goodness in his creation. Therefore, based on the teachings of Scripture, we can rightly say that God's power, wisdom, and goodness are all communicable attributes.

Belgic Confession

In the first article of the Belgic Confession we read these words: "There is one only simple and spiritual Being, which we call God . . . he is eternal, incomprehensible, invisible, immutable, infinite, almighty, perfectly wise, just, good, and the overflowing fountain of all good." This article summarizes the attributes of God with ten terms. The first six are commonly associated with God's incommunicable attributes. The remaining attributes—almighty, perfectly wise, just and good—are commonly identified with God's communicable attributes.

Like the Augsburg Confession, the Belgic Confession mentions that God is almighty—God has power—that he is wise, and that he is good. However, it also adds one more attribute when it says that God is just, or "righteous" as it may be translated. In support of this communicable attribute, the Scriptures frequently speak of God as just or righteous in places like Psalm 7:9. Passages like Hosea 12:6 and 2 Timothy 3:16 teach that human beings can be "just" or "righteous" on a creaturely scale. So, in addition to power, wisdom, and goodness, it's certainly appropriate to count justice as a communicable attribute of God.

Westminster Shorter Catechism

To the fourth question in the Westminster Shorter Catechism, "What is God?" the Catechism answers: "God is a Spirit, infinite, eternal, and unchangeable, in his being, wisdom, power, holiness, justice, goodness, and truth." The last seven of these divine perfections are communicable: God's being, wisdom, power, holiness, justice, goodness, and truth.

Like the Augsburg Confession and the Belgic Confession, the Shorter Catechism mentions wisdom, power, and goodness. It also reflects the Belgic Confession by including justice, but the Shorter Catechism adds the being or existence of God, the holiness of God, and the truth or faithfulness of God as well. Passages like Genesis 1:1 and John 1:3 make it clear that the being or existence of creation is secondary and dependent on God's being, but we still exist. According to Ephesians 4:24, holiness is also a quality of God that is reflected in various aspects of creation, including human beings. Likewise, in Scriptures like Psalm 25:5, truth or faithfulness is not only a perfection of God, but it is also granted to human beings.

> God can communicate to us certain attributes of his being, his love, his compassion, his holiness, his justice. Probably the simplest description of this is in the Westminster Shorter Catechism: "What is God? God is Spirit, infinite, eternal, and unchangeable" (incommunicable attributes) "in his being, wisdom, power, holiness, justice, goodness, and truth" (communicable attributes). We can participate with him in the latter attributes, but it is not ours to be infinite, eternal, or unchangeable. We glorify him for his infinite, eternal, and unchangeable greatness in which we do not participate, just as we glorify him for allowing us to participate in his character—his being, his wisdom, his power, his holiness, his justice, his goodness, and his truth. **Sanders L. Willson**

These lists are representative of Protestant evangelical outlooks on these matters. Still, we should add that these documents don't contain every communicable attribute. Individual theologians have often referred to other communicable attributes as well. For instance, as we mentioned earlier, it's common to see God's knowledge listed. In passages like Colossians 1:10, we find that both God and human beings exhibit knowledge. The mercy of God is often counted in this class of divine perfections because the Scriptures make it clear, in places like Luke 6:36, that both God and human beings are merciful. Of course, in passages like Deuteronomy 7:9, the Scriptures also stress the love of God as a communicable attribute.

SYSTEMATIC ORGANIZATION

As we've seen, different representative historical documents and leading theologians have listed God's communicable attributes in different ways. Unfortunately, this variety often leads inexperienced students to struggle over which list of these divine attributes is correct. In reality, there's an underlying organization to the communicable attributes of God, and this logical organization helps us see that there is actually a great deal of unity among evangelicals on how God is like us.

In chapter 7, we saw that human beings, more than any other creature, have the privilege of being like God. For this reason, the Scriptures often describe God in terms of human characteristics. This biblical focus on the similarities between God and humanity has been crucial to organizing the communicable attributes of God in systematic theology. The Bible doesn't give us a list of the communicable attributes of God; we infer them from the Scriptures. So, the way we understand people directly affects the way we organize God's communicable attributes.

We all know that modern sciences like biology, anthropology, psychology, and sociology have offered many different ways of understanding what it means to be human. Some of these modern perspectives have much to offer; others misconstrue the true nature of humanity. However, as we mentioned in chapter 7, traditional systematic theology has concentrated on three similarities between human beings and God: our intellectual abilities, our volitional capacities, and our moral character. This threefold assessment of what it means to be made in the image of God has deeply influenced how systematic theologians have organized the communicable attributes of God.

We can easily see how God's wisdom, power, and goodness mentioned in the first article of the Augsburg Confession align with these three broad categories. Wisdom deals with the mind of God and represents God's intellectual attributes, power deals with the will of God and represents God's volitional attributes, and goodness deals with God's moral attributes.

Much the same can be said of the four communicable attributes listed in the Belgic Confession. The term *wise* falls into the category of God's intellectual attributes. *Mighty* represents God's volitional attributes. The terms *just*, or *righteous*, and *good* represent God's moral attributes.

The fourth answer of the Westminster Shorter Catechism follows a similar pattern. After the somewhat unusual category of God's being or existence, wisdom represents God's intellectual attributes, power represents God's volitional attributes, and God's moral attributes include his holiness, justice, goodness, and truth.

These observations illustrate that although these historical documents aren't exactly the same, they don't represent significantly different points of view. Despite their variety, they all focus on God's communicable perfections based on three main characteristics shared by God and human beings as the image of God.

This threefold organization also helps us to assess variations introduced by individual theologians. For instance, adding God's knowledge to the wisdom of God is simply a way of distinguishing two facets of his intellectual attributes. Adding the term *sovereignty* alongside the more traditional term *power* distinguishes two aspects of God's volitional attributes. Similarly, adding terms like *mercy* and *love* distinguishes various moral attributes of God.

In this light, we can say with confidence that there is remarkable unity in evangelical systematic theology over what should be considered a communicable attribute of God. Although it's always possible to expound upon these perfections in different ways, with rare exception, God's communicable attributes tend to fall into the same three broad categories.

EXPECTATIONS OF GOD

Unfortunately, when some well-meaning followers of Christ learn about the communicable attributes of God, they misinterpret how God acted in biblical times, and they create false expectations for their own lives. God's attributes are always true of him. They don't turn on and off. They never change. Yet this doesn't mean that all God's communicable attributes are obvious to everyone every moment of every day. To have biblical expectations of God, we need to keep in mind a distinction that we've mentioned a number of times in this series—the distinction between God's attributes and his historical manifestations.

Any inability to see God's wisdom, love, power, and so on in creation is more a problem of human perspective than of God himself. One of my much-needed reminders from Scripture comes in Psalm 73. The psalmist begins with a lament about the prosperity of the rich and wicked, but in a turning point about halfway through the psalm, he says, "These things were perplexing until I entered the sanctuary of God, and then I perceived their end" (see Ps. 73:16–17). Augustine talks about the need for the healing of the soul, because sin has done such a number on us—we think, process, and understand things awry because our souls are in need of God's healing, and only when God does a work in us can we perceive and interpret properly. So the issue is not with God, it's with our perception. As a person draws nearer to God, he or she begins to see more clearly how these ideal attributes and God's workings unfold. But it's not God's problem; it's ours.
Bruce L. Fields

As we've seen, all God's attributes, including his communicable attributes, are without limits, unbound by time, and free of all variation, but as God engages his finite, temporal, and changing creation, he manifests his attributes in different ways. Some of these manifestations extend over significant periods of time; some occur only at certain places and times; but general revelation and the record of biblical history reveal that God displays his attributes in ways that are never entirely predictable.

Think of how this is true of all three traditional categories of communicable attributes. God's intellectual attributes are always true of him. He is always all-knowing and wise, but sometimes we have trouble discerning his knowledge and wisdom. This is why some biblical figures acknowledged with joy what God had revealed to them, while others longed for more understanding of the mind of God.

In much the same way, God's volitional attributes never vary. He is always powerful, and his great displays of power are often easy to see. But throughout biblical history, and in our own lives as well, it has often been hard for human beings to recognize his power. This is why biblical characters sometimes lifted their voices in praise for God's mighty deeds, but at other times they cried out for God to reveal his power.

The same can be said of God's unchanging moral attributes. God is always good, holy, just, true, loving, merciful, and gracious. But while we often perceive his goodness, at other times his goodness is difficult to comprehend. This is why so many biblical characters offered thanksgiving for the blessings they received, while others lamented over the troubles and trials they endured.

As these variations demonstrate, distinguishing God's communicable attributes from the ways he manifests these attributes in history is crucial to having the right expectations of God.

IMITATION OF GOD

The Scriptures never call people to try to imitate or resemble the incommunicable attributes of God. They don't exhort us to be infinite, eternal, or unchangeable. On the contrary, the Scriptures call for us to humble ourselves in worship and adoration of God because he's so wondrously different from us in these ways. At the same time, the practical implications of God's communicable attributes go in a different direction. Of course, we're to adore God for these perfections, but time and again, the Scriptures also call on us to imitate the communicable attributes of God.

For example, Jesus said, "Be merciful, just as your Father is merciful" (Luke 6:36). Paul gave similar instructions when he wrote, "Be kind and compassionate to one another, forgiving each other, just as in Christ God forgave you" (Eph. 4:32). Imitating the goodness of God in his mercy, kindness, and compassion is the standard of goodness for all who follow Christ. In a similar way, Peter exhorted his readers, "Just as he who called you is holy, so be holy in all you do; for it is written: 'Be holy, because I am holy'" (1 Peter 1:15–16). Peter interpreted the frequent call to holiness found in the book of Leviticus as a call for us to be like God.

Scripture is clear that God is holy, and in 1 Peter we are called to be holy because he is holy. When we are being holy by turning from sin and being separate from the world, we are not only doing what God has called us to do but reflecting a vital characteristic of God to other people. When the world looks at us and sees our holiness—that we're set apart—they see that most important characteristic of God's nature. Scripturally speaking, we are to be holy because God is holy, and we do that not only to please the Lord but also to reflect his character. **Matt Carter**

In both the Old and the New Testaments, God calls his people to be holy as he is holy, and so the holiness of God has tremendous practical importance to God's people in every age.

Holiness involves at least two things. On the one hand, it means to be "separate from" something, and in this case it means to be separate from sin. As God's people, we are called not to have anything to do with sin. But, on the other hand, it means to be conformed to God morally, to be like him as much as any creature can be like God. And so we strive in all that we do, wherever God places us, in the whole range of our relationships and employments and activities, to be like God, to reflect his character, in all that we say and do. **Guy Waters**

In terms of the three main categories of God's communicable attributes, we're to conform our minds to the mind of God; we're to conform our wills to the will of God; we're to conform our moral character to the moral character of God. However, we have to be careful here. As we've seen, God manifests his intellectual, volitional, and moral attributes in different ways as he engages his creation. In many respects, the same should be true for everyone who seeks to imitate God. To think God's thoughts after him means different things in different circumstances. To exercise our wills as God would have it, we must act in different ways at various times. To reflect the moral character of God requires us to live in the right ways at the right times.

For this reason, God's faithful people must learn to imitate God in the light of all that he has commanded in Scripture. The Scriptures provide us with countless instructions to guide us as we live our daily lives. We learn how to display the wisdom of God in various circumstances by applying everything the Bible teaches. We learn how to imitate the power of God in different circumstances by studying the many ways we're called to exercise our will in obedience to God. We learn how to imitate the goodness of God in different situations by taking account of all the moral instructions of Scripture. We submit ourselves to the various teachings of Scripture with the full confidence that the Holy Spirit is at work in our lives, preparing us for the day when we will be fully conformed to Christ. As the apostle John wrote, "We know that when [Christ] appears, we shall be like him, for we shall see him as he is. Everyone who has this hope in him purifies himself, just as he is pure" (1 John 3:2–3).

As difficult as it may be to understand, God is very different from every aspect of his creation, but he is also like us in many ways. His communicable attributes are much more than mere theory. As we grasp this facet of the doctrine of God, we understand more deeply who God is, and we also understand more fully the kind of people God wants us to be every day of our lives.

KEY TERMS AND CONCEPTS

intellectual attributes
moral attributes
technical terms
theological propositions
volitional attributes

REVIEW QUESTIONS

1. Why are technical terms so useful in theology?
2. What are some challenges to inferring theological propositions from Scripture?
3. Why do the Scriptures so frequently describe God with human characteristics?
4. What is the best guide to help us as we seek to imitate God?

DISCUSSION QUESTIONS

1. What are some possible ways that we might misinterpret how God acted during biblical times based on God's communicable attributes? (Or, why is it necessary to distinguish between God's attributes and the manifestations of his attributes?)
2. How can we continue to believe that God is good when God's goodness is often difficult to comprehend?
3. What would be the danger of attempting to imitate or resemble God's incommunicable attributes?
4. Why is it important to acknowledge that systematic theology is designed to create a faithful summary of the concepts in Scripture, not the vocabulary of Scripture?

FOR FURTHER STUDY

Bavinck, Herman. *Reformed Dogmatics*. Edited by John Bolt. Translated by John Vriend. 4 vols. Grand Rapids: Baker Academic, 2003–8.

Bray, Gerald. *The Doctrine of God*. Downers Grove, IL: InterVarsity Press, 1993.

Lewis, C. S. *The Four Loves*. London: Geoffrey Bles, 1960.

Reymond, Robert L. *A New Systematic Theology of the Christian Faith*. Nashville: Thomas Nelson, 1998.

Urban, Linwood, and Douglas N. Walton, eds. *The Power of God*. New York: Oxford University Press, 1978.

CHAPTER QUIZ

https://thirdmill.org/quiz?GOD8

PART TEST

https://thirdmill.org/quiz?GOD3s

PART 4

THE TRINITY

A history professor went to an academic social gathering and noticed a small group of physicists talking enthusiastically with each other. Curious, he wandered over to join the conversation. He knew their topic must be important by their animated responses, and some of the concepts sounded familiar, but he soon realized that he understood very little about what they were discussing. So, he politely smiled, nodded his head, and looked for an opportunity to talk with someone else.

This is how many of us feel when we hear theologians talking about the Trinity. Nearly every Christian in the world has heard of the Trinity. Yet all too often we have to admit that we understand very little about it. Still, Christians have affirmed the Trinity as a central doctrine of our faith. It distinguishes us from other monotheistic religions and sets us apart from a number of Christian cults. Although we may only grasp the basic contours of this complex teaching, the Trinity deeply shapes every other belief we hold.

9

WHAT IS THE TRINITY?

From the outset, we should note that the word *Trinity* does not appear in the Scriptures. It derives from the common Latin term *trinitas* (meaning "triad") that corresponds with the Greek term *trias*. In Christian theology, these words appeared as technical theological terms during the second century AD and came to have highly specialized significance over the centuries.

It's common to hear the doctrine of the Trinity summarized in this or similar ways: "God is one and God is three." This summary is true enough, but it often causes confusion because it gives the impression that this teaching is a bold contradiction. To avoid this impression, theologians have worked hard to distinguish in what sense God is one and in what sense he is three. Faithful Christian theologians through the centuries have put it this way: "God is one essence and three persons."

CONFESSIONS AND CATECHISMS

This distinction between the essence and persons of God has been so widespread that we can find it in any number of creeds, catechisms, and confessions. For the sake of simplicity, we'll set the stage for our discussion by drawing attention to the three highly regarded summaries of Protestant teachings that we've mentioned in earlier chapters: the Augsburg Confession, the Belgic Confession, and the Westminster Shorter Catechism.

The first article of faith in the Augsburg Confession states the doctrine of the Trinity in this way: "There is one Divine Essence which is called and which is God . . . and yet there are three Persons, of the same essence and power, who also are coeternal, the Father, the Son, and the Holy Ghost."

Article 8 of the Belgic Confession expresses the doctrine in this way: "According to this truth and this Word of God, we believe in one only God, who is one single essence, in which are three persons, really, truly, and eternally distinct . . . namely, the Father, and the Son, and the Holy Ghost."

Answer 6 of the Westminster Shorter Catechism also expresses the distinction between one essence and three persons with these words: "There are three persons in the Godhead; the Father, the Son, and the Holy Ghost; and these three are one God, the same in substance, equal in power and glory."

All three of these statements affirm that God is one substance or essence. They also affirm that God is three persons: Father, Son, and Holy Ghost (or Holy Spirit). Admittedly, these statements differ in some minor ways, and similar variety appears in other important historical formulations. So we should not expect Christians everywhere to express every aspect of the doctrine of the Trinity in precisely the same way. Nevertheless, all of these documents affirm that God is one *essence* or *substance* and three *persons*. This distinction is vital to the doctrine of the Trinity.

The classic language for the doctrine of the Trinity is one God in three persons—one substance in three persons. This is the great revelation of the Scriptures. There's only one God, not three. One God. But this one God reveals himself in terms of Father, Son, and Holy Spirit, the three persons—not three people, but the three persons of the one God. The Father sends the Son. The Son, after his death and resurrection, goes to the Father and they send the Spirit. It doesn't mean the Trinity suddenly began in the creation. No, we can go back before the creation. God was already Father, Son, and Holy Spirit, one God in three persons. Then in the creation, God interacts with the world as Father, Son, and Holy Spirit. **Justyn Terry**

ONE ESSENCE

To understand what we mean by "one essence" we have to recall our discussion in chapter 3. There we saw that the term *essence* is borrowed from Neoplatonic and Aristotelian philosophies. The word *essence* derives from the Latin term *essentia* (corresponding to *ousia*—the Greek term meaning "being"). In Latin theology, God's essence was also closely associated with the term *substantia* or "substance." As modern people, we are unfamiliar with the significance of these terms. Yet in their day, patristic and medieval theologians used these terms to refer to the unchanging reality of God that underlies all his various manifestations in history—what God is, what he always has been, and what he always will be. We also noted earlier that theologians have insisted that God's essence is one or "simple." Unlike creation, God's eternal, infinite, and unchangeable spiritual essence is indivisible and without parts.

As mere creatures, we have difficulty even imagining such things. We have glimpses of insight because God has revealed some facets of the perfections or attributes of his essence. Yet what God actually is *in himself* remains mysterious. No matter how hard we try, the nature of God's being is far beyond our grasp.

The emphasis of the doctrine of the Trinity on the one essence of God affirms, in the strongest terms, the clear biblical teaching that Christ's followers are monotheists. Opponents of the Christian faith often accuse us of believing in three gods: the Father, the Son, and the Holy Spirit. Yet, throughout the ages, true Christians have insisted that there is one God and that this God is one. He alone deserves all our humble worship and praise.

THREE PERSONS

While we affirm without hesitation that God is one essence, the doctrine of the Trinity also refers to God as three. As we have just seen, the Augsburg Confession, the Belgic Confession, and the Westminster Shorter Catechism all state that this one God is three persons. Every Christian is familiar with the names of these three persons from the New Testament: the Father, the Son, and the Holy Spirit. Still, we must ask why we speak of these three as *persons*. What is the significance of this term?

The Scriptures do not explicitly declare that the Father, Son, and Holy Spirit are persons. The term *person* is another technical theological term, derived from the Latin word *persona*. This terminology was adopted for two main reasons. In the first place, the Scriptures consistently portray the Father, Son, and Holy Spirit as having characteristics that we commonly associate with human persons. Biblical authors did not depict the members of the Trinity as unthinking, inanimate objects or forces. Rather, the biblical witness treats the Father, Son, and Holy Spirit as persons.

The personal character of the Father, Son, and Holy Spirit is closely related to God's communicable attributes—ways in which we are like God. As we saw earlier in this volume, it has been common throughout the history of the church to categorize God's communicable attributes in terms of his intellectual, volitional, and moral perfections. Leading theologians have described the personhood of the Father, Son, and Holy Spirit in slightly different ways. Yet on the whole, the Scriptures portray the Father, Son, and Holy Spirit as persons who think, make choices, and possess moral qualities.

In the second place, theologians have also spoken of the Father, Son, and Holy Spirit as persons because the Scriptures describe them as distinct from each other. Time and again the persons of the Trinity interact with each other as individuals. As just one example, immediately after Jesus's baptism, the Spirit of God descended on him, and the Father said from heaven, "This is my Son, whom I love; with him I am well pleased" (Matt. 3:17). On many occasions in the

New Testament, the Father interacts with the Son, and the Father and Son interact with the Spirit, demonstrating that they are distinct from each other. As article 8 of the Belgic Confession comments on the New Testament's consistent teaching: "It is evident that the Father is not the Son, nor the Son the Father, and likewise the Holy Ghost is neither the Father nor the Son. Nevertheless these persons thus distinguished are not divided nor intermixed."

God's essence is not somehow divided among the persons of the Trinity. God is one undivided Being. The Augsburg Confession highlights this perspective by noting that all three persons are "of the same essence and power" and are "coeternal." Every incommunicable and communicable divine attribute is fully shared by all three persons of the Trinity. All the attributes of God's essence are equally true of the Father, Son, and Holy Spirit.

Understanding what the word *person* means when we talk about the triune God is incredibly mysterious. We need a kind of placeholder to say "three . . . something," but we really don't know exactly what. In part, that's because we often get the order of the analogy between divine and human persons reversed. We tend to project human persons onto God, because that's what we know. But, of course, the reality is the reverse. God's personhood is what should define ours. And so we need to acknowledge that we don't know and can't possibly contemplate the fullness of what it means to be a person of the triune God.

To think as biblically as we can about this reality, we would turn to certain New Testament passages where Father, Son, and Holy Spirit speak to and about each other. Scripture speaks of the different persons as being in one another and loving one another, speaking and being spoken to and being spoken about. There is a reciprocal self-consciousness of the persons within the Godhead. **Daniel Treier**

If all this does not leave you dumbfounded, then you probably haven't understood it yet. The Trinity baffles us because there is nothing in creation that compares. God is not, as it is popular to say, like water that changes from solid to liquid to gas. Nor is he like the shell, the white, and the yolk of an egg. Rather, the doctrine of the Trinity teaches that God is one divine essence and three eternally distinct persons. Now, it is evident that we simply cannot understand much about this teaching. So, why do we believe it? Faithful Christians follow the example of Christ himself by believing what the Scriptures teach, even when they go beyond our understanding. As we are about to see, this longstanding outlook on the Trinity is the best way to draw together everything that the Scriptures teach about God.

KEY TERMS AND CONCEPTS

one essence
three persons
Trinity

REVIEW QUESTIONS

1. What do we mean when we say that God is one essence?
2. How can we say that God is three persons if there is only one God?
3. Why is it important to acknowledge that the members of the Trinity are coeternal?

DISCUSSION QUESTIONS

1. Why is the Trinity such an important doctrine if the term is never used in Scripture?
2. Why is the doctrine of the Trinity so difficult to understand?
3. How does the simplicity of God help us understand that God can't be divided into three parts?
4. Why is it important to acknowledge the personal character of the Father, the Son, and the Holy Spirit?

FOR FURTHER STUDY

Augustine. *On the Trinity*. Edited by Philip Schaff. Peabody, MA: Hendrickson Publishers, 1995.

Beisner, E. Calvin. *God in Three Persons*. Wheaton, IL: Tyndale, 1984.

Berkhof, Louis. *Systematic Theology*. New ed. Grand Rapids: Eerdmans, 1996.

Bloesch, Donald G. *The Battle for the Trinity: The Debate over Inclusive God Language*. Ann Arbor, MI: Servant Publications, 1985.

Erickson, Millard J. *Christian Theology*. Grand Rapids: Baker Book House, 1983.

Frame, John M. *The Doctrine of God*. Phillipsburg, NJ: P&R Publishing, 2002.

Harris, Murray J. *Jesus as God*. Grand Rapids: Baker Book House, 1992.

McGrath, Alister E. *Understanding the Trinity*. Grand Rapids: Zondervan, 1988.

Mikolaski, S. J. "The Triune God." In *Fundamentals of the Faith*, edited by C. F. H. Henry, 59–76. Grand Rapids: Zondervan, 1969.

CHAPTER QUIZ

https://thirdmill.org/quiz?GOD9

10

REVELATION OF THE TRINITY

It is one thing to grasp the basic idea of the Trinity, but it's quite another to see how this belief is based on God's revelation. When did God reveal that he is one essence and three persons? Where can we discover this teaching?

GENERAL AND SPECIAL REVELATION

From the outset, we should admit that it's not possible to infer the doctrine of the Trinity from general revelation without the help of Scripture. Although natural theology plays a crucial role in theology proper, it provides little help as we reflect on the Trinity. Thomas Aquinas rightly argued that natural theology leads believers, and even many unbelievers, to the conclusion that there is one God, but we must turn primarily to special revelation to learn that God is one essence and three persons.[1]

Still, we have to be careful even when we look for the Trinity in God's special revelation in Scripture. The Old Testament alone does not clearly lead us to the doctrine of the Trinity. As we saw earlier, the Old Testament Scriptures teach that God is one (Deut. 6:4). In

---

1. Thomas Aquinas, *The Summa Contra Gentiles*, 1.3.2.

many passages, the Old Testament also speaks of God in ways that give rise to distinctions between the Father, Son, and Holy Spirit. Yet it is only in the fuller revelation that came through Christ and the New Testament that we find the clear revelation of the three distinct persons of the one God. Christ and his apostles and prophets affirmed every teaching of the Old Testament, but they also disclosed many things about God that were unknown before their time, including the fact that the one God of Israel is three persons.

Our understanding of the triune God takes place through what we call *progressive revelation*, where God, throughout the canon of Scripture, progressively reveals more and more about who he is and how he functions.
Danny Akin

B. B. Warfield (1851–1921), rightly put it this way: "The mystery of the Trinity is not revealed in the Old Testament; but the mystery of the Trinity underlies the Old Testament revelation."[2] Warfield went on to compare the Old Testament to a room that's richly furnished but poorly lit. He noted that the New Testament introduces better lighting. It doesn't change what was in the room, but it enables us to see more clearly things that were already revealed in the Old Testament.

Everyone familiar with the New Testament knows at least several passages that speak of the Trinity. Perhaps the best-known passage is Jesus's command to baptize "in the name of the Father and of the Son and of the Holy Spirit" (Matt. 28:19). Much like Jesus's baptism formula, the apostle Paul blessed the Corinthians in this way: "May the grace of the Lord Jesus Christ, and the love of God, and the fellowship of the Holy Spirit be with you all" (2 Cor. 13:14). Paul also called for unity in the church at Ephesus by referring to the three

2. Benjamin B. Warfield, "The Biblical Doctrine of the Trinity," in *The Works of Benjamin B. Warfield*, vol. 2, *Biblical Doctrines* (Grand Rapids: Baker Book House, 2003), 141–42.

persons of the Trinity when he said, "There is . . . one Spirit . . . one Lord . . . one God and Father of all" (Eph. 4:4–6).

Still, we have to admit that even the New Testament doesn't explicitly state that God is one essence and three persons. It took centuries for the Christian church to determine that this was the best way to summarize everything the Scriptures teach about God. The details of this history go far beyond this study. It will suffice to say that influential theologians proposed different perspectives on New Testament teachings about the Father, Son, and Holy Spirit, but many of these proposals were found to be wanting. The doctrine of the Trinity as we now know it was clarified in the First Council of Nicaea (AD 325), the First Council of Constantinople (AD 381), the Council of Ephesus (AD 431),[3] the Council of Chalcedon (AD 451), the Second Council of Constantinople (AD 553), the Third Council of Constantinople (AD 680–681), and the Second Council of Nicaea (AD 787).[4] Out of a desire to be faithful to every teaching about God in the Old and New Testaments, these councils moved toward the full doctrine of the Trinity as the Christian church has affirmed it for centuries.

TRINITY IN THE NEW TESTAMENT

It is an arduous task to create a comprehensive summary of every New Testament teaching about the Trinity. The great number of Scriptures that come into play make it impossible for us to deal with them all in this chapter. Moreover, the interpretation of many biblical passages remains unsettled, even among those who affirm the Trinity. Still, we can point to a few crucial texts that illustrate how the Scriptures reveal the full deity of the three distinct persons of the Trinity.

3. Sometimes called the "First Council of Ephesus" to distinguish it from the nonecumenical Second Council of Ephesus in AD 449.

4. *A Select Library of Nicene and Post-Nicene Fathers of the Christian Church*, 2nd ser., vol. 14, *The Seven Ecumenical Councils*, ed. Henry R. Percival (1900; repr., Grand Rapids: Christian Classics Ethereal Library, 2005).

Father

It would be difficult for anyone to deny that the Scriptures teach that the Father is God. Jesus affirmed this perspective when he said, "My Father, whom you claim as your God, is the one who glorifies me" (John 8:54). He taught his disciples to pray, "Our Father in heaven" (Matt. 6:9). Three times the apostle Paul spoke of "the God and Father of our Lord Jesus Christ" (Rom. 15:6; 2 Cor. 1:3; Eph. 1:3). Time and again the Scriptures call God the Father.

What does the designation "Father" mean? In biblical times, both in Israel and outside Israel, it was common to speak of kings as fathers. This name for God revealed his paternal care for his people, but it also designated him as the King of creation. By calling God "Father," biblical authors highlighted God's royal, fatherly authority.

God is called our Father as a way to communicate something fundamentally important about his nature and the nature of his relationship to us. God creates us in community, in relationship. He creates us man and woman. He creates the human family as part of the way in which he has designed us to live. He then communicates his own relationship to us in language that makes sense of this structure, the structure of the family.

Now, part of God's design in creating marriage and the human family was to reflect, in some sense, the divine family: Father, Son, and Holy Spirit. This communal relationship, so critical to the being of God, to God's character, is reflected in the way we are to relate one to each other. This language of *Father* is, in some sense, a metaphor, but it's also more than a metaphor in that it communicates the reality that God's bond of loyalty, reflected in the way he has made us, is also part of the very community in which God lives in eternity. **Richard Lints**

Son

Time and again, the New Testament also teaches that the Son is God, equal with the Father in power and glory. One of the clearest references to the full divinity of the Son appears in the opening chapter of John's gospel: "In the beginning was the Word, and the Word was with God, and the Word was God. He was in the beginning with God. All things were made through him, and without him was not any thing made that was made . . . And the Word became flesh and dwelt among us, and we have seen his glory, glory as of the only Son from the Father, full of grace and truth" (John 1:1–3, 14 ESV).

To mention just a few features of this passage, in verses 1–3 the "Word" (who is identified with "the only Son" in verse 14) was not only "with God" but "was God." The second person of the Trinity was from all eternity or "in the beginning with God." He was not created; he is the eternal Son because "all things were made through him." At the same time, however, the Word, or Son, is distinct from the Father. As verse 14 tells us, he was sent "from the Father."

Even very, very liberal scholars like Rudolf Bultmann, the great liberal New Testament scholar of the twentieth century, said that John 1:1 is absolutely undisputed. It clearly teaches the deity of Christ. The Greek means, "What God was, the Word was"—in terms of his essence, in terms of what he is, the Word is identical to God. And so the last few words of the verse—"and the Word was God"—say, in the most concise way possible, that the second person of the Trinity is equal in authority, in worship, in attributes, to the first person of the Trinity, yet they are not the same person. Does John 1:1 teach the deity of Christ? Absolutely it does. We have virtually no differences among any manuscripts whatsoever regarding this verse. John 1:1 affirms the full deity of Christ. **Daniel B. Wallace**

In a similar way, John referred to the deity of the Son in his portrait of the court of heaven: "I heard every creature in heaven and on earth and under the earth and on the sea, and all that is in them, singing: 'To him who sits on the throne and to the Lamb be praise and honor and glory and power, for ever and ever!' The four living creatures said, 'Amen,' and the elders fell down and worshiped" (Rev.

5:13–14). This passage identifies the Father as "him who sits on the throne" and the Son as "the Lamb." In so doing, John distinguished between the two. The Father and the Son are distinct persons. At the same time, however, John also set both persons apart from "every creature." They are both Creator, not created.

As these two New Testament passages and many others indicate, the Son is not the Father, but he is still the true and living God. Christ is God and we must worship and adore him for all his divine attributes.

Naturally, the incarnation of Christ raises serious questions about his deity. In the early centuries of the Christian faith, the church dealt with a number of controversies related to the divinity and humanity of Christ after he became flesh. These controversies were complex. Here, it will suffice to say that there were several outlooks on the subject. Some influential theologians argued that Christ emptied himself of his deity when he became human. Others insisted that the incarnate Christ only appeared to be human. Others urged that the divine and human natures of Christ mixed together. Still others taught that Christ switched back and forth between being divine and human.

Despite these various points of view, by the time of the Council of Chalcedon in AD 451, it was determined that the best way to represent all the teachings of the New Testament in these matters was to affirm that the incarnate Christ is two natures in one person, what was called the "hypostatic union." This is yet another mystery of the Trinity. The divine and human natures of Christ are never separated from each other. Yet his divine nature maintains all the essential attributes of God, and his human nature maintains all the essential attributes of unfallen humanity. In this sense, even after the second person of the Trinity became a full human being, he remained, and remains, the eternal divine Son of the Father.

Holy Spirit

It also took some time for the church to come to grips with New Testament teachings about the Holy Spirit. In the early centuries of Christianity, a number of influential theologians argued that the Spirit was nothing more than an impersonal force emanating from God. The same is true even today in some Christian cults. Still, by the time of the First Council of Constantinople in AD 381, it became evident that the best way to acknowledge all that the New Testament teaches about the Spirit was to affirm that he is a distinct person and that he is God.[5]

Regarding the Holy Spirit, the Apostles' Creed simply says, "I believe in the Holy Spirit," which is exactly what the Nicene Creed said when it was first written at the first ecumenical council in Nicaea in 325. But in 381 the council of Constantinople met and wrote two-thirds of the Nicene Creed that we have today, and in particular it developed the section on the Holy Spirit because people were asking questions about the Holy Spirit that hadn't been asked before. The revised Nicene Creed said, "We believe in the Holy Spirit" and added, "the Lord, the giver of life, who proceeds from the Father and the Son, and with the Father and the Son is worshiped and glorified." That text ascribed divinity to the Holy Spirit in two ways. First, it afforded divine status to the Holy Spirit when it said, "the Lord . . . worshiped and glorified." Second, it ascribed to the Holy Spirit divine attributes: "the giver of life." **Tim Foster**

A number of passages indicate that the Holy Spirit is both a person and fully divine, but for our purposes here, we'll mention only two. In the first place, the distinct personhood of the Spirit is evident because the Scriptures attribute to him the qualities of a person. For instance, the apostle Paul wrote, "The Spirit searches all things, even the deep things of God. For who among men knows the thoughts of a man except the man's spirit within him? In the same way no one knows the thoughts of God except the Spirit of God" (1 Cor. 2:10–11). Notice here that the Spirit of God "searches" and "knows" the thoughts of God. Searching and knowing are the actions of a

---

5. "Excurses on the Heresies Condemned in Canon I," in *The Seven Ecumenical Councils*, 243–48.

self-aware person. This passage resembles many other passages in Scripture where the Spirit is similarly portrayed as a distinct person, not as an impersonal force.

Not every passage that talks about the Spirit of God identifies the Spirit as a distinct person, but in John 14–16 we read about the Spirit doing things that only a person would do. For example, Jesus says that he will send another advocate like himself, the Holy Spirit, and the Spirit will prosecute the world concerning sin and righteousness and judgment, just like Jesus did. The Spirit is a witness just like we are witnesses, and so on. Thus, the Spirit is identified as a distinct person in a number of passages. **Craig S. Keener**

The fact that the Bible teaches that the Holy Spirit is a distinct, divine person and not just a mode of expression of the one God or a phase of his manifestation is very, very significant for the Christian life. For one thing, it means that we are indwelt by a person, not an impersonal force. A person is indwelling us, to whom we may relate, who is in an everlasting relationship with the Father and the Son.

I'm struck by how, in his account of Jesus's baptism, Luke goes out of his way to tell us that when the Holy Spirit came from heaven and descended upon Jesus in the form of a dove, he came in bodily form. Reading the other gospel accounts, you could have made the argument that this was a visible manifestation—maybe a vision or something else without substance. Well, you can't say that after you've read the gospel of Luke.

One of the great old sixteenth-century commentators made the point that the reason that Luke draws attention to the fact that the Holy Spirit came in bodily form is to emphasize that all the persons of the Trinity were present at the baptism of Jesus and that those persons are not forces or powers. They're persons. God the Father is speaking. God the Son is being baptized. God the Spirit is present in bodily form. The idea is that these three persons relate to one another personally and to us personally. It makes all the difference in the world to have a relationship with another person rather than to feel the power of a force. **J. Ligon Duncan III**

In addition to teaching that the Spirit is a distinct person, the New Testament also freely identifies the Holy Spirit with God himself. As just one example, when Peter confronted Ananias over his lie (Acts 5:1–11), he first said to him, "Ananias, how is it that Satan has so filled your heart that you have lied to the Holy Spirit" (Acts 5:3). Still, when Peter confronted Ananias a second time, he said, "You have not lied to men but to God" (Acts 5:4). Lying to the Spirit was the same as lying to God because the Spirit *is* God. Throughout the Scriptures, the names, attributes, works, and worship associated with the Holy Spirit indicate that the Spirit is the same divine essence as the Father and the Son.

Certain works demonstrate the deity of the Holy Spirit, and I'll briefly mention four. First, in John 16 we're told that the Spirit judges. Judgment is a prerogative that belongs only to God. Second, Psalm 33:6 says that the Spirit is involved in creation. The act of creating is something only God can do. Third, in John 3 we see that the Spirit regenerates, that he brings about the new birth, which is something that only God can do. Fourth and finally, we know from 2 Timothy 3:16 that the Spirit inspires the Scriptures. Only God can reveal himself to us. Together these factors point to the deity of the Holy Spirit. **Keith Johnson**

The deity of the person of the Holy Spirit raises an astonishing fact that must not escape us. The New Testament frequently speaks of the Spirit dwelling among us and within us, and this means that God himself dwells among and within us. We should be overwhelmed with humility and praise for the honor that God has bestowed on us.

EQUALITY AND SUBORDINATION

So far, we've stressed how the New Testament reveals that the Father, Son, and Holy Spirit are distinct persons of one divine essence who share fully and equally in the glory of every essential divine attribute. Yet we fall short if we stop there. The New Testament also speaks in many places of subordination within the Trinity. Nowhere do the Scriptures teach that the Father submits to the other persons of the Trinity. Yet they often speak of the Son as subordinate to the Father and the Spirit as subordinate to the Father and the Son.

From the early centuries of our faith until our own day, followers of Christ have had difficulty balancing these teachings. Still, the mainstream of Christian theology has acknowledged that even though the Father, Son, and Holy Spirit are equal, there is also subordination among the persons of the Trinity.

A number of recent systematic theologians have sought to clarify these matters by distinguishing two outlooks: ontological and economic perspectives on the Trinity. Many have questioned the value of making this distinction, but it remains a popular and helpful way of summarizing the equality and subordination of the persons of the Trinity.

Ontological Trinity

On the one side, we may speak of the "ontological Trinity," or better "an ontological perspective" on the Trinity. The philosophical term *ontology* refers to the being or essence of God and focuses on the eternal relations among the persons of the Trinity. It has also been dubbed *Trinitatis ad intra* in Latin—meaning "the Trinity toward the inside"— because it refers to the relationships between the Father, Son, and Holy Spirit apart from their works of creation and providence.

As we've seen, traditional systematic theologians have rightly maintained that the Father, Son, and Holy Spirit are one essence, but they have also recognized distinctions among the persons of the Trinity from all eternity. The Westminster Confession of Faith (1647) describes these relationships in ways that echo many creeds, confessions, and catechisms: "The Father is of none, neither begotten, nor proceeding; the Son is eternally begotten of the Father; the Holy Ghost eternally proceeding from the Father and the Son."[6]

6. Westminster Confession of Faith, chapter 2.3.

Father. The Confession emphasizes first that the Father is "of none, neither begotten, nor proceeding." This claim is clear enough. There is no indication in the New Testament to the contrary. The Father always has and always will have royal, paternal authority within the Trinity.

Son. The ontological perspective on the Trinity also emphasizes that, "the Son is eternally begotten of the Father." This teaching is often designated the "eternal generation" of the Son. It draws from Scriptures that speak of him as the "only begotten" Son, using the Greek term *monogenēs* (John 1:14, 18; 3:16, 18; 1 John 4:9). Now, terminology like "eternally begotten" is so unfamiliar in our day that it easily gives the impression that the Son is somehow begotten over and over, but this is not the case. It simply means that the Son has forever been the Son. As such, the eternal generation of the Son stands in opposition to false teachers who have claimed that the Son was created or made. As the Council of Nicaea put it, the Son is "begotten, not made, being of one substance with the Father."[7] As passages like Revelation 5:13–14 teach, the Son is eternal. He has always been, is, and always will be the Son of the Father.

Holy Spirit. In much the same way, the ontological perspective on the Trinity also speaks of "the Holy Ghost eternally proceeding from the Father and the Son." This way of describing the Spirit draws from biblical passages like John 15:26 that speak of the Spirit proceeding or coming from the Father. Now, Western and Eastern Christians have disagreed over whether the Spirit proceeds from the Father and the Son or from the Father alone. Yet both traditions have agreed that the Spirit proceeds eternally. The language of "eternal procession" is also unfamiliar. It often leads modern Christians to think that the Spirit proceeds over and over. Yet this is not what it means. It opposes false teachers who have argued that the Spirit

---

7. Philip Schaff, ed., *The Creeds of Christendom, with a History and Critical Notes* (1877; repr., New York: Harper & Brothers, 1919), 1:28.

began to emanate from God at some point in history. This formulation was simply designed to acknowledge that the Holy Spirit has always been, is, and always will be the Spirit.

> The first person has always been the Father of his Son, and his Son has always been the Son of his Father, and that goes back forever. And there has always been the Spirit of the Father and the Spirit of the Son, and the three are inseparable. They're always with each other—and not only *with* each other but *in* each other (the Son is in the Father, the Father is in the Son, and so on). They interpenetrate, so there are not three different gods. There is only one Godhead, one divine nature that is indivisible and three persons. **Paul R. Raabe**

Economic Trinity

While the ontological equality of the persons of the Trinity is vital to the Christian faith, modern systematic theologians have also spoken of an economic perspective to account for the fact that the New Testament teaches subordination within the Trinity. The term *economic* derives from the Greek term *oikonomia*, which signifies household management, assignments, or roles. This outlook is also known as *Trinitatis ad extra* in Latin, meaning "Trinity toward the outside." It refers to the personal subordination of the Son to the Father, and of the Spirit to the Father and the Son, in relation to the works of creation and providence.

It would be difficult to deny that the New Testament stresses this perspective on the Trinity. Time and again, the Scriptures emphasize the economic subordination of the Son to the Father. Jesus himself summed up his role in history as one of obedience to the Father: "I have come down from heaven not to do my will but to do the will of him who sent me" (John 6:38). Along similar lines, Jesus also spoke of economic subordination of the Holy Spirit when he referred to "the Counselor, the Holy Spirit, whom the Father will send in my name" (John 14:26).

The ontological and economic perspectives are helpful ways of expressing two truths about the persons of the Trinity that the New Testament affirms. The Father has always been the Father; the Son has always been the Son; the Holy Spirit has always been the Holy Spirit. These three persons share equally in the glory of every essential divine attribute from all eternity. Yet in the course of creation and providence, the Son submits to the Father's role for him, and the Holy Spirit serves in the role given to him by the Father and the Son.

There's only one Trinity, but we need to talk about it in two different ways because a couple of statements by Jesus raise some questions. Jesus says in John 10:30, "I and the Father are one," and the people around him clearly understand what Jesus is saying, because they take up stones to stone him. When Jesus asks them why, they say, "Because you, being a man, make yourself God." But in John 14:28, Jesus says, "The Father is greater than I." That's perplexing!

We resolve this by talking about the first statement as referencing the ontological Trinity and the second the economic or the functional Trinity. The ontological Trinity focuses on the nature of God, his essence, and the Father and the Word and the Spirit all share the same nature. We say, "God the Father, God the Son, God the Holy Spirit." That's ontological. It has to do with the nature of being.

The economic Trinity, however, has to do with function. It resides in the *person*, so different persons can have the same nature but function differently. Thus, the Son can say, "The Father is greater than I" only in function, in that the Father sends the Son.

The idea of ontological Trinity and economic Trinity is very important because it helps us to understand how could Jesus say, "I and the Father are one" and "The Father is greater than I." His statements are wonderfully explained by understanding the difference between economic Trinity and ontological Trinity. **Bruce Little**

In this chapter we've only sketched the basic contours of the doctrine of the Trinity. The Trinity is complex because it represents the efforts of faithful Christians to account for everything that the Bible teaches about God. It is mysterious at every turn because it takes us to the limits of human understanding. Still, the doctrine of the Trinity protects us from one of the greatest dangers we all face: the tendency to highlight some biblical teachings about God to the neglect of others. The Trinity reminds us that God has condescended to give us glimpses into who he is. Still, it also reminds us that we are mere creatures who serve an unfathomable Creator.

KEY TERMS AND CONCEPTS

economic Trinity
eternal generation
eternal procession
Father
Holy Spirit
ontological Trinity
Son

REVIEW QUESTIONS

1. How would you explain the full deity of the Son from Scripture?
2. How would you defend the full deity of the Holy Spirit from Scripture?
3. What does the ontological Trinity teach us about the unity of the Godhead?
4. What does the economic Trinity teach us about the individual roles of each member of the godhead?

DISCUSSION QUESTIONS

1. Why do we need to have both the ontological and economic perspectives on the Trinity?
2. What do we mean when we say that the Son is eternally begotten of the Father?

3. What is the significance of the eternal procession of the Holy Spirit from the Father and the Son?
4. How would the Christian faith be altered if either the Son or the Holy Spirit were somehow less than fully divine?
5. Why is it important to acknowledge that the Holy Spirit is a person?

FOR FURTHER STUDY

Bavinck, Herman. *Reformed Dogmatics.* Vol. 2, *God and Creation,* edited by John Bolt. Translated by John Vriend. Grand Rapids: Baker Academic, 2004. See pages 95–334.

Bray, Gerald. *The Doctrine of God.* Downers Grove, IL: InterVarsity Press, 1993.

Haykin, Michael. "Defending the Holy Spirit's Deity: Basil of Caesarea, Gregory of Nyssa, and the Pneumatomachian Controversy of the 4th Century." *Southern Baptist Journal of Theology* 7, no. 3 (Fall 2003): 74–79.

Palmer, Edwin. *The Holy Spirit: His Person and Ministry.* 2nd ed. Phillipsburg, NJ: P&R Publishing, 2005. See chapters 1–8.

Poythress, Vern S. *Knowing and the Trinity: How Perspectives in Human Knowledge Imitate the Trinity.* Phillipsburg, NJ: P&R Publishing, 2018.

Reymond, Robert L. *Jesus, Divine Messiah: The New Testament Witness.* Phillipsburg, NJ: Presbyterian and Reformed, 1990.

Warfield, Benjamin B. "The Biblical Doctrine of the Trinity." In *Biblical Doctrines.* Vol. 2 of *The Works of Benjamin B. Warfield.* Grand Rapids: Baker Book House, 2003.

———. *The Lord of Glory.* New York: American Tract Society, 1907. Reprint, Grand Rapids: Baker Book House, 1975.

———. "The Spirit of God in the Old Testament." In *Biblical and Theological Studies,* edited by Samuel G. Craig, 127–56. 1950. Reprint, Philadelphia: Presbyterian and Reformed, 1952.

CHAPTER QUIZ

https://thirdmill.org/quiz?GOD10

PART TEST

https://thirdmill.org/quiz?GOD4s

PART 5

GOD'S PLAN AND WORKS

At one time or another, many of us have made big plans for the future, plans for what we hope to accomplish in life. Small children often imagine that fantastic things are in store for them. Young adults frequently set grandiose goals, but the older we get, the more obvious it becomes that we may succeed in fulfilling *some* of our plans, but not all of them. In the final analysis, we simply don't have the forethought or the ability to accomplish everything we want to do.

In many respects, the very opposite is true of God. The Bible reveals that God has a plan, but unlike the plans we make, God's plan will not fail. In the final analysis, he has the forethought and the ability to accomplish everything he wants to do.

11

GOD'S PLAN FOR HISTORY

As you'll recall, under the influence of Hellenistic philosophies, patristic and medieval theologians typically gave top priority to identifying and explaining the perfections of God's essence. The same has been true for most evangelical systematic theologians throughout the centuries. However, God's attributes aren't the only focus of theology proper. The doctrine of God has also given a great deal of attention to God's plan and to how he fulfills his plan.

When it comes to the attributes of God and the Trinity, evangelicals hold many, if not most, beliefs in common, but the same cannot be said when it comes to the plan of God. This topic has been quite divisive because it touches on controversial issues like divine foreknowledge and predestination. Well-informed evangelicals have held very different outlooks on these topics, and it's unlikely that there will ever be complete agreement on them. For this reason, our goal is to discuss these matters, as much as possible, in ways that promote mutual understanding and respect among various evangelical groups.[1]

---

1. The author and editors hold to the traditional Reformed view of these subjects.

BIBLICAL PERSPECTIVES ON GOD'S PLAN

In systematic theology, the expressions *plan*, *decree*, and *decrees of God* have had rather specific and consistent technical meanings. The Scriptures, however, use several different Hebrew and Greek expressions related to this same theological concept in a variety of ways. They speak directly of God's plan or plans, but they also refer to his purpose, his counsel or decrees, his will, and his good pleasure. We have in mind the Old Testament families of Hebrew words related to *ḥāšab* (usually translated "to think," "to plan," or "to determine"); *zamam* (usually translated "to purpose" or "to plan"); *yā'aṣ*, (meaning "to give counsel" or "to decree"); *rāṣôn* (usually rendered "pleasing" or "favorable"); and *ḥāpēṣ* (also translated "pleasing"). We should also add the New Testament Greek terms: *boulē* (often rendered "purpose," "counsel," "decree," or "will"); *prothesis* (usually translated "purpose" or "plan"); *thelēma* (meaning "will" or "desire"); and *eudokia* (which is usually translated "pleasure").

In contrast with the ways technical terms are used in systematic theology, these and similar expressions in the Bible aren't always used in specific and consistent ways. As we've said, the Scriptures often use very similar terminology to signify different concepts, and they also use different terminology to signify very similar concepts. In fact, the meanings of these and other closely related Hebrew and Greek terms often overlap in the Scriptures. They also appear in various combinations with each other and are used interchangeably at times. So we have to be careful to assess the meanings of these terms in specific biblical contexts.

Divine Immanence

We've already said that it's important to affirm the mystery that God is both transcendent and immanent. He transcends the limitations that characterize creation because he is infinite, eternal, and unchangeable, but this does not mean that God is disconnected from or uninvolved with his creation. On the contrary, the Bible also teaches that God is immanent. He condescends and fully engages his finite, temporal, and changing creation. When we survey the Scriptures, we discover that biblical authors spoke of God planning in association with both his transcendence and his immanence.

There is an immanence—a nearness and a closeness—that God wants to have as part of his relationship with his creation and with his people. Sin obviously affects that, but it doesn't mean that God suddenly disappears. Before the fall, God walks with Adam and Eve in the garden. Later in the Old Testament, he sets up a tabernacle to be with his people. In the New Testament, we see God's immanence more in terms of the incarnation—"The Word became flesh and dwelt among us" (John 1:14 ESV). So we see the Lord's desire to be in his creation, to be with his people in his desire to dwell with his people in the tabernacle and his desire to be with his people through Christ's incarnation. He longs to be with us; he longs to be with his creation. **Scott Manor**

Consider God's own words regarding his immanent engagement with creation: "If at any time I announce that a nation or kingdom is to be uprooted, torn down and destroyed, and if that nation I warned repents of its evil, then I will relent and not inflict on it the disaster I had planned" (Jer. 18:7–8). Here, God spoke of something he had "planned" using the Hebrew verb ḥāšab, meaning to "think," "plan," or "determine." Now, in many circles, when Christians hear of God having a "plan," they automatically assume that the Bible refers to something God determined to do from eternity past, but this passage doesn't speak of God planning in this way. On the contrary, this plan of God is cast in terms of his immanent involvement with creation. It is announced in response to the disobedience of a nation or kingdom. It is God's plan for such a nation to be punished and overthrown. More than this, God explicitly declared that this plan could be reversed. If a nation repents of its evil, God may relent and not carry out the disaster he had planned. The Scriptures often report that God makes such historical plans—plans that come and go as he interacts with his creation.

Along these same lines, Luke referred to the "purpose" of God: "The Pharisees and experts in the law rejected God's purpose for themselves, because they had not been baptized by John" (Luke 7:30). Luke referred to God's "purpose" by using the Greek term *boulē*, meaning "purpose," "counsel," "decree," or "will," but the "purpose," "counsel," "decree," or "will" of God in view in this passage is associated with God's immanence, not with his transcendence. His divine purpose rose within a particular historical setting as the Pharisees and experts in the law were called to be baptized by John, and this purpose was "rejected" when they refused to submit to this decree.

Now consider Paul's words about the "will" of God: "Give thanks in all circumstances, for this is God's will for you in Christ Jesus" (1 Thess. 5:18). Paul referred to God's "will" using the Greek term *thelēma*, but notice, once again, that this verse is not oriented toward God's transcendence. Rather, in this passage, the will of God is Paul's specific instruction: "Give thanks in all circumstances."

Theologians often call these types of biblical instructions the "prescriptive will of God," or God's "prescribed" commands. Throughout biblical history, God required his people to obey his will. There are hundreds, perhaps thousands, of places in Scripture where God called his people to think, to act, and to feel in certain ways. These declarations of the prescriptive will of God always conformed to God's infinite, eternal, and unchanging moral character, but God expressed his prescriptive will as he engaged his people in different ways at different times. In addition, the prescriptive will of God is often unfulfilled because his creatures disobey what he commands.

As just one other example, notice what Jesus said about his own "will" or desires: "O Jerusalem, Jerusalem, you who kill the prophets and stone those sent to you, how often I have longed to gather your children together, as a hen gathers her chicks under her wings, but you were not willing" (Matt. 23:37). Jesus said, "I have longed" using the term *thelō*, which is the verbal form of the noun *thelēma*. This passage does not refer to God's transcendence. Many times in history God longed, desired, or willed to protect his children from their oppressors, but his desire was not fulfilled because the people were not willing.

The Scriptures often speak of God making plans, having purposes, giving counsel, issuing decrees, willing, and being pleased, as factors of his immanent, historical interactions with creation. These historical plans of God are finite, temporal, and quite often changeable.

Divine Transcendence

As we've just seen, the Scriptures frequently speak of God's planning in the context of his immanent interactions with creation, but this is only half the picture. The Scriptures also speak of God's plan in ways that reflect the fact that he is transcendent—that he is infinite, eternal, and unchangeable. When Scripture speaks of God's plan in this way, it refers to what theologians often call the "decretive will of God"—what God has ordained as a firm decree, something that will happen without fail.

Consider how God referred to his purpose and pleasure when he was speaking in terms of his transcendence: "I make known the end from the beginning, from ancient times, what is still to come. I say: My purpose will stand, and I will do all that I please" (Isa. 46:10). It isn't difficult to see that this passage depicts God's plan in ways that stand in sharp contrast to his historical engagements with creation. God spoke of his "purpose" (from the verbal root yā'aṣ), and he talked of doing all that he pleased (from the Hebrew term ḥāpēṣ), but he did so in the context of his eternal decrees, which are aspects of his transcendence rather than of his immanence. He spoke of the fact that he makes the end known "from the beginning," referring to his eternality, and he made it clear that his purpose is unchanging and that it cannot fail. We find a similar outlook where Job confessed to God, "I know that you can do all things; no plan of yours can be thwarted" (Job 42:2).

This association of God's plan with his transcendence also appears in Paul's well-known words "In him we were also chosen, having been predestined according to the plan of him who works out everything in conformity with the purpose of his will" (Eph. 1:11). Several key Greek terms appear in this passage. Paul referred to God's "plan" (*prothesis*), "purpose" (*boulē*), and "will" (*thelēma*). Notice Paul's orientation toward God's transcendence. First, the "plan" in view here is not narrowly focused but all encompassing; it includes "everything." Second, the plan does not develop in historical circumstances; it is eternal. We read that all who were "chosen" in Christ had been "predestined" according to God's plan. This outlook echoes Ephesians 1:4, where Paul said that God had chosen his people in Christ "before the creation of the world." Third, the plan of God in view here cannot be thwarted. It's unfailing because God "works out everything" in conformity with his "purpose" (*boulē*) and "will" (*thelēma*).

In Acts 2:23, the term *boulē* is also rightly translated as God's "deliberate plan." In this verse, Peter said that Jesus was handed over to the Romans "by God's deliberate plan." Similarly, in Acts 4:28, *boulē* is translated as God's "will" when the church prayed about what God's "power and will had decided beforehand should happen." The same word is translated "purpose" in Hebrews 6:17 where the author of Hebrews referred to "the unchanging nature of [God's] purpose."

Jesus himself spoke of God's decretive will in this way: "This is the will of him who sent me, that I shall lose none of all that he has given me, but raise them up at the last day. For my Father's will is that everyone who looks to the Son and believes in him shall have eternal life, and I will raise him up at the last day" (John 6:39–40). Jesus referred to his Father's "will" using the Greek term *thelēma*. However, this wasn't a command from God that could be disobeyed. Rather, Jesus focused on God's will as something that would certainly come to pass. God willed or decreed that Jesus would lose none of those given to him. Specifically, the Father willed that everyone he had given to the Son would believe in the Son and receive eternal life. This will of God is his sovereign decree. It cannot be frustrated; it cannot be overturned.

Sometimes the Scriptures associate God's planning, purpose, counsel, decree, will, and pleasure with his immanence—his limited, temporal, and changing interactions with creation. At other times, they use very similar terminology with a focus on God's infinite, eternal, and unchangeable transcendence over his creation. Therefore, if we hope to be biblical in our understanding of God's plan, we must find ways to affirm both of these perspectives.

> God's eternal plan must be immutable because God is immutable, meaning that he is unchanging. God's immutability says to us that he's unlike us; he doesn't have to learn, grow, or develop over time. And since he is unchangeable, everything that emanates from him as it relates to his eternal plan has to be unchangeable also. Thus, even before Adam and Eve's sin in the garden, Christ had already, before the foundations of the earth, become the Passover Lamb who ultimately would atone for sin. God's plan, because of who he is, is unchangeable, and his eternal will is being accomplished.
> **Larry Cockrell**

THEOLOGICAL POSITIONS

Sadly, many well-meaning Christians have emphasized only one or the other of the two ways that the Scriptures speak of God's planning. Some have stressed mainly God's immanence; others have emphasized mainly his transcendence. In the past, it would have been relatively easy to associate these emphases with particular Protestant denominations. Yet in recent history, many lines separating denominations have faded, and these traditional orientations have all but disappeared. Because of this shift, we won't speak here in terms of what one branch of the church or another believes. We'll simply sketch some general tendencies that exist across denominational lines today.

Extreme Outlooks

One of the core values of traditional systematic theology has been to create logically coherent summaries of what the Scriptures teach on every topic. Theologians have worked hard to reach this goal as they have explored what the Scriptures teach about the plan of God. Unfortunately, sometimes the desire for logical consistency has led to extremes.

Fatalistic theology. On the one side, many well-meaning followers of Christ are inclined toward what we may call "fatalistic theology." Fatalistic theology has taken different forms, but on the whole, it explains everything that happens in history almost exclusively in terms of God's transcendent plan. Now, as we've seen, some biblical passages support the belief that God's plan, purpose, counsel, decrees, will, and pleasure reflect his transcendence. In this sense, everything that has ever occurred or ever will occur has been ordered by the all-encompassing, eternal, and unfailing plan of God. However, fatalism falls short of the full range of biblical teaching on this subject. It fails to give due weight to the development of God's plans, purposes, counsel, decrees, will, and pleasure as he interacts with his finite, temporal, and changing creation.

I am not a fatalist. I believe that what I do counts. That's why there's a judgment seat. I believe I know what I'm doing. I'm not a robot. I'm actually doing what I'm doing. But I also believe that God is not limited by my actions. He is able to take my obedience and my disobedience and still solve his purposes. "God is sovereign, and he draws straight lines with crooked sticks." I may be a crooked stick, but he can still get his line drawn. We have confidence not that God is so powerful that he turns us into robots but that his power is so majestic that he creates us as free moral agents. That is the doctrine of the sovereignty of God. Free moral agency does not put God on the puppet string of humanity, nor does the sovereignty of God put us on a puppet string. God sovereignly ordains our choices and accomplishes his purposes through what we are doing. **Harry L. Reeder III**

If we were to have a conversation with someone who tends toward fatalistic theology, we might find that they answer several key questions in these ways:

"Does God plan something and then set it aside while interacting with creation?"

Fatalists tend to say, "Never."

"Is God's counsel or decree ever frustrated?"

In the fatalistic view, "Of course not."

"Can the will and pleasure of God ever be thwarted?"

Fatalists tend to reply, "Impossible."

In addition, when the Bible seems to indicate other responses to these questions, fatalists argue that Scripture merely describes events as they appear to human beings, not as they truly are.

Open theology. On the opposite extreme of the spectrum from fatalism, other theologians have adopted a position that has come to be known in recent decades as "open theology." There's a lot of variety among open theologians, but on the whole, this point of view explains nearly everything that happens in history in terms of God's immanence. We've seen that there's biblical support for believing that God forms many different plans as he engages his creation. In this sense, as God interacts with the finite, temporal, and changing world, his historical plans, purposes, counsel, decrees, will, and pleasure don't always come to fruition. However, open theology takes this biblical teaching to an extreme and fails to give due weight to God's eternal, all-encompassing, unfailing plan. Many who hold to this extreme view agree that a few events have been set in place by God's infallible, eternal decrees. They often acknowledge that major events like the first advent of Christ, the time of his glorious return, and the final outcome of history are fixed by God's sovereign will. Other than these few events, open theologians usually maintain that the success of God's plans, purposes, and will are entirely dependent on history, especially on the choices that spirits and human beings make.

If we were to engage open theologians in conversation, they would tend to answer a few key questions in these ways:

"Does God have an all-encompassing, eternal, and unfailing plan for history?"

Open theology says no.

"Are God's counsel and decrees ever frustrated by human rebellion?"

In this view, "It's almost always possible."

"Can the will and pleasure of God ever be thwarted?"

Open theology replies, "Quite often."

From this extreme point of view, when Scripture indicates that God has an eternal, unfailing plan, open theists insist that it refers to only a few select events.

Open theology—or, as it's sometimes called, open theism—holds a view called *presentism* that argues that God knows everything about the past, everything about the present, and much about the future, but not about any free human decisions or anything that depends on free human decisions.

Believers in all major Christian traditions throughout the history of the church have disagreed with this view and affirmed that God knows the future exhaustively. Psalm 139 talks about God's knowing what is on our tongues before we even open our mouths and speak. Scripture contains predictions and their fulfillments, especially in 1 and 2 Kings. Isaiah 40–48 gives great teaching about how Yahweh distinguishes himself from the gods of the nations, especially through his knowledge of the future. In the New Testament, Jesus assures us that our Father knows our needs before we even ask. He demonstrates his knowledge of the future by predicting his own passion, his death and suffering. When Jesus predicts both Peter's denial and Judas's betrayal, he tells his disciples, "I have told you this before it happens so that when it does happen, you'll know that I am he." That is a claim for his own deity.

Would God base such strong evidence for his own unique deity in the Old Testament and the New Testament on something uncertain, if God only could *predict* things that happen in the future, as opposed to exhaustively know them? For these reasons, believers in all major traditions have affirmed that God knows the future exhaustively, in opposition to the teachings of open theism. **Steven C. Roy**

Centrist Outlooks

It's fair to say that in one way or another the mainstream of formal evangelical systematic theology has affirmed both sides of what the Scriptures teach about God's plan. Centrist outlooks agree that God has an all-encompassing, eternal, and unfailing plan for what happens in history. They also affirm with equal strength that as God engages his creation he forms many plans that are limited in scope, temporal, and changing. It's not that only one or the other is true. Rather, unlike those who have tended toward the extremes, the majority of evangelical theologians have insisted that both perspectives are true.

When we embrace the ways the Scriptures speak of God's planning, both in association with his transcendence and with his immanence, we face some of the greatest mysteries of the Christian faith. Human beings can understand these matters as far as God has explained them in Scripture, but we can never grasp them in ways that solve every conundrum, or in ways that answer every question that could be raised. Instead, it's wise to approach this issue much like we do the Trinity and the two natures of Christ. Rather than attempting to resolve every mystery involving God's plan, we should learn all we can about both sides of these biblical outlooks and admit that our human understanding is limited.

If we were to have a conversation with theologians who hold to more centrist evangelical outlooks on God's plans, they would tend to answer some key questions in these ways:

"Does God have an all-encompassing, eternal, and unfailing plan for history?"

"Yes."

"Does God make specific plans as he involves himself in the course of history?"

"Yes."

"Will the *eternal* plan, purpose, counsel, decrees, will, and pleasure of God be accomplished without fail?"

"Yes."

"But can God's *historical* plans, purposes, counsel, decrees, will, and pleasure be thwarted?"

"Yes."

In other words, the mainstream of evangelical theology has sought to reflect both sides of the teachings of Scripture. It affirms both God's transcendent, eternal plan and his immanent, historical plans. While these centrist outlooks have characterized the mainstream of evangelical systematic theology, there have been differences among those who endorse them.

Order of eternal decrees. When systematic theologians refer to the order of God's decrees, they have in mind the logical order of the elements involved in God's eternal plan for history. What are the interconnections among the major decrees that God ordained before his first act of creation? Did he decree one particular decree before he decreed another? These kinds of questions have often been directed at God's eternal decrees regarding humanity's fall into sin and redemption in Christ. There have been many answers to these kinds of questions, but on the whole it has been customary to group them into three categories.

In the first place, we should mention "supralapsarianism" (from the Latin terms *supra*, meaning "above," and *lapsus*, meaning "the fall"). As this name implies, God's decree to save his people should be placed above—or before—his decree to permit the fall of humanity into sin. In this view, the order of God's eternal decrees can be summarized in this way:

1. the decree to save God's chosen people (and to bring judgment against all others)
2. the decree to create
3. the decree to permit the fall into sin
4. the decree to accomplish and offer redemption through Christ
5. the decree to apply redemption in Christ to true believers

In the second place, we should mention "infralapsarianism" (from the Latin terms *infra*, meaning "beneath," and *lapsus*, meaning "the fall"). As this name implies, God's decree to save his people should be placed beneath—or after—his decree to permit the fall of humanity into sin. In this view, the order of God's eternal decrees can be summarized in this way:

1. the decree to create
2. the decree to permit the fall into sin
3. the decree to save God's chosen people
4. the decree to accomplish and offer redemption through Christ
5. the decree to apply redemption in Christ to true believers

In the third place, we should mention a view that is often called "sublapsarianism" (from the Latin terms *sub*, meaning "under," and again *lapsus*, meaning "the fall"). This view is sometimes considered a subcategory of infralapsarianism. As the name implies, God placed his decree to save his people under—or after—his decree to permit the fall of humanity into sin, but in this view, the decree to save came after God's decree to offer redemption, not before. This outlook can be summarized in this way:

1. the decree to create
2. the decree to permit the fall into sin
3. the decree to accomplish and offer redemption through Christ
4. the decree to save God's chosen people
5. the decree to apply redemption in Christ to true believers

It's important to realize that, for the most part, these different points of view developed to help theologians to address *other* sorts of theological questions like: "How can we maintain that God is good when his plan permits humanity's fall into sin and only grants salvation to some?" "How can God's offer of the gospel to all people be genuine when God has an all-encompassing, eternal, and unfailing plan?" "How can we affirm the moral responsibility of human beings when God is sovereign over their actions?" These are important questions. Still, most leading evangelical theologians recognize that the Scriptures don't give us enough information to identify the logical order of God's eternal decrees. There is even some question as to whether or not his decrees can be ordered in a simple, linear fashion. So, by and large, while centrist evangelicals still tend to favor one view over another, most of us have rightly concluded that these matters involve a great deal of speculation. They are largely beyond what God has revealed in Scripture.

When one speaks of the order of decrees, usually such discussion is generated out of an attempt to provide a kind of logical order to the way God does things. Before there was "time," God already existed, so we can only speculate because we just don't know what that looks like to God. That's why the best theologians, when they talk of the order of decrees, aren't so much talking temporal sequence as logic, as coherence. In that framework, this is a way of talking about things in order to accommodate all that Scripture says about God and the fall and the sequence of God's plans and so on, in a logical sense, without it being a sequence in a temporal sense, in order to be faithful to the witness of Scripture. **D. A. Carson**

Eternal decrees and foreknowledge. More often than not, when systematic theologians discuss the relationship between God's eternal decrees and his foreknowledge, they highlight three New Testament passages. Acts 2:23 speaks about the crucifixion of Christ occurring according to "God's deliberate plan and foreknowledge"; 1 Peter 1:2 refers to God's elect who have been "chosen according to the foreknowledge of God"; and Romans 8:29 says that "those God foreknew he also predestined." It's clear that these passages point to interconnections between God's eternal decrees and his foreknowledge. By and large, evangelicals have handled these passages in two ways.

On the one side, many have held that God's foreknowledge was the basis of his decrees. In other words, in eternity God knew the course that history would take. He understood how events would unfold—including his engagements with the choices that spirits and human beings would make. On the basis of this foreknowledge, he decreed the eternal plan by which all events would unfold without fail.

On the other side, many evangelicals have held that God's decrees are the basis of his foreknowledge of history. In this view, God planned or decreed everything that would happen in history simply according to his own good pleasure, and this unfailing plan gave God foreknowledge of everything that would happen in history.

The debates over these matters are often motivated by other theological concerns, such as the goodness of God and the free agency of human beings. They also involve disagreements over whether biblical references to God's foreknowledge focus on God's mere foreknowledge of events or his personal, loving foreknowledge of the people that he has chosen for salvation.

Regardless of these differences, we can all agree on some things. Do the Scriptures teach that God foreknows everything? Yes. Do the Scriptures teach that God has foreordained everything, including eternal salvation? Yes. So, as much as we may favor one of these outlooks over the other, in the end we should all admit that God's decrees and his foreknowledge go hand in hand in many different ways. Moreover, we must always keep in mind that we're discussing God in eternity, so our normal ways of thinking don't necessarily apply. To be dogmatic about the relationship between God's decrees and foreknowledge is to go beyond what the Scriptures reveal.

As John Calvin argued, "We, indeed, place both doctrines [of foreknowledge and eternal decrees] in God, but we say that subjecting one to the other is absurd."[2] Calvin was well known for his firm belief in God's sovereignty over all of history. As he pointed out here, the Scriptures don't spell out precisely how God's foreknowledge and eternal decrees relate to each other, so it's absurd to subject one to the other.

Ultimately, whenever we consider the plan of God, we must

---

2. John T. McNeill, ed., *Calvin: Institutes of the Christian Religion*, trans. Ford Lewis Battles (Philadelphia: Westminster Press, 1960), 3.21.5.

remember that both divine transcendence and immanence are crucial to the Christian life. God is sovereign over every trial and trouble in life. Everything in life takes place as God has ordained. At the same time, God is intimately involved with our lives. He turns history in one direction and then in another direction, often depending on the choices we make. If we deny either of these views, we rob ourselves of some of the most vibrant, life-giving teachings of Scripture.

One of the perennial questions in theology has to do with the relationship between divine sovereignty and human freedom, between the choices that we make and the ultimate will and purposes of God. Many theologians emphasize one side more than the other side. The really great theologians teach both sides in their biblical fullness, but, regardless of our views, there is something that we can learn from one another.

People who emphasize human choice may minimize the biblical passages that talk about the sovereignty of God and how all-encompassing it is and how everything that happens ultimately is the purpose of God. But people who really like to emphasize the sovereignty of God may minimize the real choices that people make and the significance of those choices for what happens in the world. It's tempting for all of us to gravitate toward the passages that agree with our theology and to explain away or minimize the passages that may support someone else's view. The more that we engage in theological dialogue with one another, the more we help each other see the significance of every passage of Scripture and really wrestle with its implications. **Philip Ryken**

KEY TERMS AND CONCEPTS

centrist outlooks
decretive will
fatalistic theology
foreknowledge
God's plan

open theology
order of God's eternal decrees
prescriptive will

REVIEW QUESTIONS

1. Why is it important to acknowledge that God has an eternal plan for all of history?
2. How can we avoid fatalism in our theology?
3. What are the dangers of open theology?
4. How significant are the logical order of God's eternal decrees for Christian theology?
5. What do theologians mean by the foreknowledge of God?

DISCUSSION QUESTIONS

1. Why does a centrist outlook on God's plan require both God's transcendence and his immanence?
2. How would you express your own view of God's eternal plan from Scripture?
3. How would you express your own view of the relationship between God's foreknowledge and his eternal decrees?
4. Is it possible that God's eternal plan could ever change?

FOR FURTHER STUDY

Basinger, David, and Randall Basinger, eds. *Predestination and Free Will: Four Views of Divine Sovereignty and Human Freedom*. Downers Grove, IL: InterVarsity Press, 1986.

Bavinck, Herman. *Reformed Dogmatics*. Edited by John Bolt. Translated by John Vriend. 4 vols. Grand Rapids: Baker Academic, 2003–8.

Boettner, Loraine. *The Reformed Doctrine of Predestination*. Grand Rapids: Eerdmans, 1957.

Carson, D. A. *Divine Sovereignty and Human Responsibility: Biblical Perspectives in Tension*. Grand Rapids: Zondervan, 1994.

Craig, William Lane. *The Only Wise God: The Compatibility of Divine Foreknowledge and Human Freedom*. Grand Rapids: Baker Book House, 1987.

Pink, Arthur W. *The Sovereignty of God*. Grand Rapids: Baker Books, 1930.

CHAPTER QUIZ

https://thirdmill.org/quiz?GOD11

12

GOD'S WORKS OF CREATION AND PROVIDENCE

The Scriptures strongly focus on what God has done, what he is doing and what he will do in the history of the world. The importance of these themes in the Bible has led to their importance in theology proper as well. In the doctrine of God, systematic theologians explore the fundamental characteristics and patterns that underlie all God's works. Throughout the centuries, systematic theologians have divided God's engagements with creation into two main parts: his work of *creation* and his work of *providence*.

CREATION

Systematic theologians have focused a lot of attention on the moment when God created *ex nihilo* or "out of nothing." Passages like Genesis 1:1, John 1:3, and Hebrews 1:2 indicate that nothing apart from God ever existed until God brought it into existence. Evangelicals have rightly rejected all forms of polytheism (the belief that gods or godlike forces joined with God in the work of creation), pantheism (any identification of God with his creation), and dualism (the belief that what we call creation has actually existed from all eternity alongside God). Instead, evangelical systematic theology has consistently maintained the biblical distinction between God as the Creator and his creation.

Systematic theology has also dealt with the twofold division between heaven and earth that God established in creation. This division appears in Genesis 1:1 where we're told that God created the heavens and the earth, and it has persisted. In the New Testament, Paul described the division this way: "For by [Christ] all things were created: things in heaven and on earth, visible and invisible" (Col. 1:16). Here, Paul affirmed the distinction between heaven and earth, and then expounded on it by describing heaven as invisible and earth as visible. This distinction has been so central to Christian theology that it has been included in a number of important creeds and confessions that speak of God as the Creator of all things, visible and invisible.[1]

Now, even though God created the invisible heavens and visible earth as distinct realms, he never intended them to be completely separate. Rather, through his reign over all creation, he holds both sides of this twofold division in unity. As he revealed to the prophet Isaiah, "Heaven is my throne, and the earth is my footstool" (Isa. 66:1). This passage succinctly explains an outlook that runs just beneath the surface of every page of Scripture. In effect, creation is God's cosmic palace or temple, with invisible heaven above and visible earth below.

In the Old Testament, Israel's temple was modeled after this twofold arrangement of creation. It had an inner, elevated chamber known as the most holy place, or the holy of holies. This chamber represented God's reign in the upper, invisible realms of creation. This elevated chamber was surrounded by lower levels of the temple known as the holy place and the outer court or courtyard. Both of these lower levels represented the lower, visible realms of creation.

This basic twofold outlook helps us understand God's grand

---

1. For example, in the Nicene Creed and Westminster Confession of Faith, chapter 4.1.

purpose for his creation. Simply put, the goal of history is that God's glorious reign in the upper, invisible world will extend downward and spread to every corner of the visible world. In the end, God's visible glory will fill all of creation so that every creature, above and below, will worship him forever. This basic outlook underlies everything that the Bible tells us about God's work of creation.

> The goal of human history is for the whole earth to be transformed into the visible and immanent temple, garden, realm, throne of God. This is the very same purpose with which the Bible opens in Genesis 1 and 2—that God made a world that was very good, but he made a garden in which his presence was immanent and visible, and it was a holy place. The man and the woman were told to spread the garden to the whole world by multiplying, by filling it, and by subduing it. In the fall, that program is interrupted, yet in the promise in the garden—that a seed of the woman would bruise the serpent's head—that promise is ultimately fulfilled. And so the earth becomes a place where the glory of God is not hidden any longer. Rather, the earth is filled with the glory of God. **Michael J. Glodo**

Invisible Dimensions

Modern materialism has influenced followers of Christ so much that many serious students of theology pay little attention to what the Bible teaches about the invisible dimensions of creation. To be sure, many believers become overly preoccupied with what remains largely unseen, but in academic study, we have to guard against the opposite extreme. Much of God's plan for his creation is initiated and furthered by what takes place in the invisible realms. So, as we study the doctrine of God, we must take into account what theologians often call the "preternatural world."

The primary biblical terms for the invisible dimension of creation are *šāmayim* in Hebrew and *ouranos* in Greek. Both terms are often translated "heaven" or "the heavens," but they can also refer to what modern people call "the sky" and "outer space." In our discussion of the preternatural world, we'll focus only on the times when these terms refer to the upper realms—the realms that remain invisible to human beings, except when God grants supernatural visions of them.

Arrangement. The Scriptures don't give much detail about the arrangement of the invisible heavens, but they indicate that it is quite complex. For instance, passages like Psalm 104:3 speak of God's heavenly upper room or "upper chambers" (NASB). According to 1 Kings 8:30, and a number of other passages, this heavenly chamber is "heaven, [God's] dwelling place," or as it may also be translated, "heaven, the place of [God's] enthronement." Isaiah 63:15 describes this same heavenly palace as the place of "[God's] lofty throne, holy and glorious." In addition, in 2 Corinthians 12:2–4, Paul drew from rabbinical theology and spoke of "the third heaven," calling it a "paradise . . . [of] inexpressible things." Beyond this, Deuteronomy 10:14, Psalm 115:16, and a number of other passages refer to "the highest heavens." These and similar biblical references alert us to the fact that the arrangement of the invisible world is quite complex and goes far beyond our comprehension. Even so, these and many other verses indicate that the invisible, heavenly realms are arranged as the upper, exalted dimensions of God's cosmic palace.

Occupants. Needless to say, the most glorious of all heaven's occupants is God himself, but we have to be careful here. Many think of heaven as the place where God exists in his full transcendence, but this is not the case at all. Heaven is a part of creation. It is finite, temporal, and changing. Although heaven is above the visible world, it is nonetheless a place where God immanently engages his creation. Now, in 1 Kings 8:27, Solomon declared that God is so transcendent that "even the highest heaven cannot contain [him]," but in the same prayer, Solomon spoke of heaven as the place of God's enthronement—the place where God hears and responds to his people's prayers. Therefore, heaven is a place where God enters into the finite creation by sitting on a throne and engaging his heavenly creatures (Job 1:6–12; Dan. 7:9–11; Luke 22:31). God's heavenly throne room is exalted above the visible world, but it's nonetheless a part of his creation. From the beginning of history, when God said, "Let there be light," he has directed history as the King of creation from his heavenly court.

Of course, God isn't the only occupant of the upper, invisible realms. For instance, we know for certain that Jesus ascended in his glorified humanity to the throne of his father David, and he now sits at the right hand of God the Father in the court of heaven (Acts 2:31–33). For the most part, though, heaven is filled with spiritual creatures and the departed souls of the faithful. These occupants and their activities remain invisible apart from supernatural visions. They are called "spirits" (Matt. 8:16; Heb. 1:14), "sons of God" (Pss. 29:1; 89:6; literal translation), "holy ones" (Ps. 89:5, 7; Zech. 14:5), "messengers" (Ps. 91:11; Dan. 4:13; literal translation), and "armies" or "hosts" (Ps. 148:2; Dan. 8:10). Some of these spirits are assigned responsibility for nations on earth (Ps. 82). Gabriel and Michael are prominent angelic leaders, especially serving God on behalf of his chosen people. Cherubim serve as guardians of God's holiness, and seraphim minister before the throne of God.

Scripture tells us that all the heavenly spirits were first created good, like the rest of creation. Those spirits who remain faithful are called "elect angels" (1 Tim. 5:21), but other heavenly spirits rebel against God (John 8:44; 1 Tim. 3:6; 2 Peter 2:4; Jude 6). We don't know much about this angelic rebellion, except that it is widespread and that Satan—and perhaps other spirits—rebelled before the temptation of Adam and Eve. Satan, the adversary (also called the "Devil" or the "accuser"), and other evil spirits (often called "demons," "rulers," "authorities," and "powers") continue to participate from time to time in the heavenly court (2 Chron. 18:18–22; Job 1:6–12; Ps. 82). They serve at the bidding of the court of heaven and fulfill God's will on earth, though with evil intent. However, Satan and other evil spirits won't serve the court in heaven forever. Instead, a place of eternal judgment has been prepared for them in the netherworld, along with human beings who rebel against God.

When we talk about the angelic world, we think not only about heaven and its inhabitants but also the demonic powers, the fallen angels. We sometimes think that the fallen angels have more freedom than the good angels, because the good angels are under God's absolute control in heaven and they serve him, while the fallen angels get to do as much fun and as much mischief as they can on earth. But the Bible's answer is very clear: God has just as much authority over the fallen angels as he does over the good angels. Everything that they do, they do only because God has allowed it. Similarly, everything that Satan does, and everything the Beast and the Antichrist do during that final period of history (Rev. 13:5–8), they do only because God has given them permission, even to blaspheme the name of God. So, God is in total absolute control of the fallen world, and God is in absolute control of the heavenly world. **Grant R. Osborne**

Visible Dimensions

The Scriptures present all creation as God's cosmic palace or temple, but what about the physical world we inhabit? Throughout the centuries, systematic theologians have looked to the first chapters of Genesis to discern how God ordered and filled the visible aspects of his palace. The visible world was initially "formless and empty" (Gen. 1:2), but by the end of the creation week, God had completed the initial, pleasing arrangement and population of creation and was resting on his heavenly throne (Gen. 2:1–3).

Arrangement. God spent the first three days of creation ordering and arranging its formlessness. On the first day, God established day and night (or light and darkness) in the visible realms of his palace; on the second day, God established the visible sky and seas; and on the third day, God established dry land and plant life on the floor of his cosmic palace.

Occupants. God spent the next three days filling creation's ordered arrangement with occupants. Now, at times, occupants of the invisible heavens appear in the visible world to serve the purposes of the divine King in heaven. The Bible also reports numerous theophanies (visible appearances of God himself) in biblical history. He appeared to Adam and Eve in the garden of Eden. He appeared in dreams and visions and in the pillar of smoke and fire to Israel. And of course, God appeared through the incarnation of Christ and his earthly ministry. However, the first chapter of Genesis focuses primarily on the ordinarily visible occupants of the physical world.

God divided the light and darkness on the first day. On the fourth day, he placed the sun, moon, and stars to occupy and govern the day and night. On the second day, God established the visible sky and seas, and on the fifth day he created birds and sea creatures to inhabit them. On the third day God established dry land and plant life, and on the sixth day, he placed animals and human beings there.

All these occupants of the visible world play important roles in God's purposes for his creation, but according to Genesis 1:26–31, only humanity has the special role of being the image and likeness of God: "God blessed them and said to them, 'Be fruitful and increase in number; fill the earth and subdue it. Rule over the fish of the sea and the birds of the air and over every living creature that moves on the ground'" (v. 28).

What does it mean for humanity, both male and female, to be created in the image of God? There's been a lot of debate amongst theologians about what this actually means, but scholars of the Old Testament are aware of a find at Tell Fakhariyah in Syria —a statue of a ruler in that region that is called "the image and likeness" of that particular ruler. This shines light upon Genesis 1. Humans, as God's image bearers, are those who are to be, if you will, statues for God, or representatives for God, who is the real King of this world. When I think "image bearers," I think those who are called to represent or to reflect God in this world as they care for creation.
Andrew Abernethy

As Genesis 2 explains, in the beginning God placed Adam and Eve in the garden of Eden. This earthly sacred garden was so perfect, so beautiful, so holy, that God would appear regularly in his visible glory. However, the goal of history was for the perfection, beauty, and holiness of the garden to extend to the far reaches of the earth. In this way, it would be appropriate for God's visible glory to appear everywhere to his endless praise. The primary instrument for this expansion of holiness and God's glory throughout the world was humanity—the image and likeness of God. By God's gracious empowerment, and the service of angels against every physical and spiritual foe, the redeemed of humanity were destined to fulfill history's purpose in service to God.

This is why Scripture and evangelical systematic theology place so much stress on the role of Christ as the perfect image and likeness of God. Not only did he pay for the sins of his redeemed people, but when Christ returns to make the new heavens and new earth, he will fill the earth with God's holy images and make all things new. God's visible glory will shine throughout the invisible and visible realms of creation so that every creature will worship God. As Paul wrote, "At the name of Jesus every knee should bow, in heaven and on earth and under the earth, and every tongue confess that Jesus Christ is Lord, to the glory of God the Father" (Phil. 2:10–11).

PROVIDENCE

The Latin theological term *providentia* speaks of God "attending to," "sustaining," or "taking care of" creation as he works out his eternal plan. As you can imagine, providence includes countless works of God because God upholds all things, all the time. Many topics within systematic theology, other than theology proper, focus on particular aspects of God's providence—especially on how God attends to sin and salvation in history. But for theology proper, the main focus has been to describe the patterns of God's providence that underlie all of history, patterns that characterize every dimension of God's care for his creation.

The word *providence* comes from the Latin and means "to see in advance" or "to see before." It ultimately represents that God is overseeing, looking over, watching over, caring for all creation. This concept of providence is tied in with a number of other important doctrines that a number of Christians have unfortunately missed in terms of their appreciation for how God cares for us. He cares for his creation, and that gives comfort. It gives a sense of God's goodness. It gives a sense that he is not a distant God or an angry God; he is a God who delights to provide, who knows what he is doing, and who is moving everything according to his purposes and plans. **Lewis Winkler**

In many branches of the church, discussions of God's providence rely on a distinction that we mentioned earlier. Traditional systematic theologians have referred to God as the "First Cause" (the ultimate cause behind everything that happens in history), and they've referred to various dimensions of creation as "second causes" (facets of the invisible and visible creation that also cause events to occur in history).

As you can imagine, the patterns of God's providence are so complex that leading theologians have held different views that go far beyond the scope of our discussion. Broadly speaking, some branches of the church have tended to emphasize God's role as the First Cause and to diminish the significance of second causes. Other branches have highlighted the importance of second causes and have diminished God's involvement in the unfolding of history. Between these extremes, there have been a number of more balanced perspectives that attempt to give due weight both to the First Cause and to second causes.

Second Causes

It's fair to say that the Scriptures affirm the significance of God's activity in history and the significance of second causes. It would be difficult to read the Bible and conclude that God has little or no impact on the course of history. Yet it would be equally difficult to conclude from the Scriptures that facets of creation, especially spirits and human beings, have little or no impact on what happens. The challenge is to describe how both of these outlooks are true. The Scriptures do not succinctly summarize these matters in one place. So, theologians have to gather information from many portions of the Bible and piece them together as coherently as possible.

One influential and helpful way of summarizing these matters appears in the fifth chapter of the Westminster Confession of Faith, "Of Providence." The second section of this chapter reads: "Although, in relation to the foreknowledge and decree of God, the First Cause, all things come to pass immutably, and infallibly; yet, by the same providence, he ordereth them to fall out, according to the nature of second causes, either necessarily, freely, or contingently."

This section of the Confession begins by affirming what we've called centrist evangelical outlooks on the plan of God. Every event in history accords with God's all-encompassing and eternal plan so that nothing is left to chance. Rather, God insures that "all things come to pass immutably, and infallibly." Yet the Confession quickly adds that God orders all things "to fall out, according to the nature of second causes." The expression "according to the nature of second causes" reflects complex debates among medieval Scholastic theologians that have focused on one central question: Are all second causes of the same nature, or do they have different qualities? The Confession acknowledges that different elements of creation have different natures. Rocks, trees, plants, animals, human beings, and spirits are different from each other, and God orders the course of history by directing these elements according to their different natures.

Sadly, a number of theologians have argued that God is not simply the First Cause of all things, but the *one and only* Cause. It is as if every element in creation is a lifeless puppet, and all historical events result from God acting directly on creation, as if he were the great Cosmic Puppeteer. In this view, if God does not directly and personally make things happen, then nothing happens. The earth revolves in its elliptical orbit around the sun solely because God causes it to move in this way. Trees grow tall because God personally causes them to grow. Animals walk about and fish swim in the sea only as God moves each one himself. In this view, human beings and invisible spirits choose to do good and evil because God makes these choices for them.

Now, it's true that God sustains all creation. Affirming the words of a Greek poet, Paul said, "In him we live and move and have our being" (Acts 17:28). However, creation doesn't simply wait until God pulls strings to make things happen. Instead, God has granted various capacities to different facets of creation so that they function in different ways as second causes of historical events. The Confession summarizes this variety in three categories: "necessarily, freely, or contingently."

The Westminster Confession says that God is the primary cause of everything but also that he makes use of, establishes, and affirms secondary causes. What does this mean? The language is very carefully chosen to affirm that what people do matters, hence the word *cause*. But God is ultimately sovereign, hence the word *secondary*. God is the primary cause. The means of grace that God has put in place—preaching, Bible memorization, evangelism, prayer, the Lord's Supper, baptism—are all secondary causes that we embrace. We plant, we water, but God gives the increase. Every farmer understands this. A farmer plants the seed in the soil, but he can't make it grow. Only God can make it grow. But God has given the farmer the means to use: the secondary causes of planting and watering. **Harry L. Reeder III**

Necessarily. The term *necessarily* refers to the ways many aspects of God's creation accomplish his purposes mechanically, or as we might say, according to the laws of nature. The radiation of the sun necessarily warms the earth. The gravitational force of the earth causes objects to fall to the ground. Chemical reactions produce predictable results. Involuntary biological processes have certain effects. The list goes on and on. Much like Genesis 8:22 speaks of the predictable cycles of cold and heat, summer and winter, day and night, God has arranged creation so that countless second causes move history toward his goals through necessary interconnections.

Freely. The term *freely* refers to functions of volitional creatures that are not mechanical. Second causes act "freely" in the sense that the outcomes of their actions are not necessarily what volitional creatures intend. As the Sovereign over all creation, God is fully in control of the outcomes. Yet second causes produce many effects that are random, inadvertent, or accidental from a creaturely point of view. For instance, Exodus 21:13 speaks of unintentional sins. First Kings 22:29–34 speaks of a time when King Ahab was struck by an arrow shot "at random." The Scriptures frequently acknowledge that the free or unintended consequences of second causes are often very significant in God's providence.

Contingently. The term *contingently* refers to the ways that the intentional choices of volitional creatures cause things to happen in history. Now, God knows all things and, in this sense, there are no contingencies from his divine perspective. However, the Scriptures stress over and over that the contingent choices of God's creatures, especially spirits and human beings, shape the course of history. In Genesis 2:17, God warned Adam that he would suffer death if he ate the forbidden fruit, and the results of his contingent choice have influenced every facet of history. Human choice is also crucial in obtaining eternal salvation from the curse of sin. As Paul put it, we will be saved "if" we declare that Jesus is Lord and "if" we believe that God raised him from the dead (Rom. 10:9).

In reality, the processes of divine providence are so complex that every set of events in history involves some combination of these interconnections among second causes. We may say that God orchestrates all history so that it unfolds according to the different natures of second causes—necessarily, freely, and contingently.

God's Use of Means

How does God engage the various second causes he has created in his providential care throughout history? Once again, the fifth chapter of the Westminster Confession of Faith offers a helpful outlook. In the third section of this chapter we read, "God, in his ordinary providence, maketh use of means, yet is free to work without, above, and against them, at his pleasure." It would be difficult to overemphasize the last phrase of this statement. God interacts with second causes "at his pleasure." He does with them what he wishes, when he wishes, and how he wishes. God is not constrained to work one way or another with second causes. Even so, this portion of the Confession also makes an important distinction between God's "ordinary providence" and how he is free to act in extraordinary ways.

Ordinary providence. One kind of interaction ordinarily characterizes God's engagements with second causes. As the Confession puts it, God "maketh use of means." To put it another way, God ordinarily works *through* the second causes he has created.

We can see this easily in the realm of the visible world. How does God nourish plants? Ordinarily, he does this through nutrients that are in the soil, through water, and through sunlight. How does God keep human beings alive? Usually, he employs food, oxygen, water, and the like. In fact, the Scriptures indicate that God even spreads the saving work of Christ throughout the world by making use of human beings as second causes: "How, then, can they call on the one they have not believed in? And how can they believe in the one of whom they have not heard? And how can they hear without someone preaching to them? And how can they preach unless they are sent?" (Rom. 10:14–15).

Even so, God doesn't merely work through visible second causes in his ordinary providence. Throughout the Scriptures, we find that God also makes use of invisible second causes: angels, demons, and even Satan himself. As the psalmist wrote, "Praise the LORD, you his angels, you mighty ones who do his bidding, who obey his word. Praise the LORD, all his heavenly hosts, you his servants who do his will" (Ps. 103:20–21).

There are countless implications of the fact that God ordinarily makes use of visible and invisible second causes in his providential care over creation. In this vein, systematic theologians often turn to the subject of theodicy: the vindication of God's goodness in view of the existence of evil. Understanding how God carries out his plan through second causes helps us grasp how God can be holy and good when evil exists in his creation. God's ordinary providence sheds light on this subject in at least two ways.

First, the Scriptures are clear that God is sovereign over evil. It is fully under his control. Passages like Job 1:6–12 indicate that God even employs Satan in his service from his heavenly throne. As Jesus explained to Peter, "Simon, Simon, Satan has asked to sift you as wheat. But I have prayed for you, Simon, that your faith may not fail" (Luke 22:31–32). This is why Jesus taught his disciples to pray, "Lead us not into temptation, but deliver us from the evil one" (Matt. 6:13). As Jesus indicated, we are to pray that God will deliver us from the evil one because God is in control of him.

When we study the divine powers in the Bible, we discover that Satan is probably the second most powerful person. But it's a great counsel to me that he's not omnipresent or omniscient—in fact, he's not *omni* anything. He's not like God.

It's not that God and Satan exist in equal power and throw one punch here, one punch there. No, Satan nowhere comes close to who God is. Often he is defeated just by prayers of believers and their power or by the unity among the believers—ways the Bible describes how Satan can be put aside. Moreover, the Holy Spirit resists him so that he's not able to function. So, yes, he's powerful, but he's limited in a great sense, and nothing comes close to the power of God. **Sukhwant S. Bhatia**

Second, God's ordinary providence indicates that God himself never directly causes evil. Rather, temptations come indirectly through evil second causes. As James insisted, "Let no one say when he is tempted, 'I am being tempted by God,' for God cannot be tempted with evil, and he himself tempts no one" (James 1:13 ESV). James gave two reasons for not blaming temptation on God. On the one side, "God cannot be tempted with evil" because God is good, and evil does not entice him in any way. On the other side, "[God] himself tempts no one." This literal translation rightly highlights what is explicit in the Greek text. God *himself* does not tempt. In other words, God does not directly tempt us toward evil. Rather, temptation to sin comes through preternatural creatures like Satan and his demons and through our own sinful propensities. As James went on to say, temptation is successful because "Each person is tempted when he is lured and enticed by his own desire (James 1:14 ESV).

God's ordinary use of second causes explains how God is sovereign over evil, but not the author of evil. While all things fall out according to his eternal plan, the responsibility for evil rests on preternatural and natural second causes that rebel against the commands of the one who made them.

Extraordinary providence. As much as we should acknowledge God's ordinary providence, we should never overlook what we may call his "extraordinary providence." As the Confession puts it, God is "free to work without, above, and against [means], at his pleasure."[2] In effect, God also engages his creation through what we often call divine interventions or miracles. Sometimes he causes events to occur "without" the use of second causes. In his immanent involvement with creation, God does things directly and personally. At other times, God causes things to occur in history that are "above" second causes. In other words, God takes things beyond their normal ends. In addition, God also works "against" second causes. God reverses the ordinary results of second causes, especially as he brings good out of evil.

The Bible highlights many examples of extraordinary providence. In the Old Testament, these special acts of providence were often designed as signs to vindicate the authority of God's representatives like kings, prophets, and priests. In the New Testament, extraordinary providence often testified to the authority of Jesus

2. Westminster Confession of Faith, chapter 5.3.

and his first-century apostles and prophets. Of course, unusual or extraordinary providence also includes other dramatic displays of God's blessings and curses, even when they are not closely associated with the authority of God's special servants.

God is always free to do things in ways that we do not expect. To be sure, when we examine our world, we see God's ordinary providence at every turn, and we should be grateful for the ways he makes use of second causes every day of our lives. At the same time, faithful followers of Christ should expect to experience God's extraordinary providence as well. We should call out for his extraordinary intervention into history, because he always remains free to work without, above, and against every facet of creation. Nothing can withstand him.

For from him and through him and to him are all things.
To him be glory forever! Amen. (Rom 11:36)

KEY TERMS AND CONCEPTS

extraordinary providence
God's works
invisible dimensions of creation
ordinary providence
visible dimensions of creation

REVIEW QUESTIONS

1. What does it mean that God created *ex nihilo*?
2. How does Scripture distinguish between the visible and invisible realms of God's creation?
3. How has God arranged the invisible dimensions of God's creation?
4. How does Scripture describe the pattern of the creation of the visible realm in terms of the first three days and second three days?
5. What do theologians mean by "second causes"?

DISCUSSION QUESTIONS

1. Why do believers today seem to focus so much on the visible realm over the invisible realm in our daily lives?
2. What examples can you see of God's use of second causes that occur necessarily, freely, or contingently?
3. How does the Bible distinguish between ordinary providence and extraordinary providence?

FOR FURTHER STUDY

Berkhof, Louis. *Systematic Theology*. New ed. Grand Rapids: Eerdmans, 1996.

Berkouwer, G. C. *The Providence of God*. Translated by Lewis B. Smedes. Studies in Dogmatics. Grand Rapids: Eerdmans, 1952.

Blocher, Henri. *In the Beginning: The Opening Chapters of Genesis*. Translated by David G. Preston. Downers Grove, IL: InterVarsity Press, 1984.

Erickson, Millard J. *Christian Theology*. Grand Rapids: Baker Book House, 1983.

Gilkey, Langdon. *Maker of Heaven and Earth: A Study of the Christian Doctrine of Creation*. Garden City, NY: Doubleday, 1959.

Helm, Paul. *The Providence of God*. Downers Grove, IL: InterVarsity Press, 1994.

Kline, Meredith G. *Images of the Spirit*. Grand Rapids: Baker Book House, 1980.

Murray, John. "Calvin's Doctrine of Creation," *Westminster Theological Journal* 17.1 (November 1954): 21–42.

Young, Davis A. *Creation and the Flood*. Grand Rapids: Baker Book House, 1977.

CHAPTER QUIZ

https://thirdmill.org/quiz?GOD12

PART TEST

https://thirdmill.org/quiz?GOD5s

COMPREHENSIVE EXAM

https://thirdmill.org/quiz?GOD

GLOSSARY

This glossary is provided as a quick reference and does not attempt a comprehensive treatment of any of the people or terms listed. Greek and Hebrew terms appear in transliteration.

'ădōnāy yhwh. Hebrew term meaning "Sovereign Lord"; often translated "Lord God."

anthropomorphism. Term referring to how God sometimes speaks or behaves in ways that seem almost human.

Aristotle (ca. 384–322 BC). Ancient Greek philosopher and scientist who studied under Plato and founded the Lyceum in Athens.

aseity. The quality of existing in and of oneself; being entirely self-sufficient.

Augsburg Confession. The foremost confession of faith of the Lutheran church, written by German Reformer Philipp Melanchthon; first presented on June 25, 1530, at the Diet of Augsburg.

Belgic Confession. Confession of faith written by Reformer Guido de Brès in 1561 in the Netherlands; one of the doctrinal standards of the Reformed Church.

boulē. Greek term for "purpose," "counsel," "decree," "will."

Calvin, John (1509–1564). French theologian and key Protestant Reformer; wrote *Institutes of the Christian Religion*.

communicable attributes. Characteristics of God that can be communicated to his creation in some measure (e.g., wisdom, power, goodness).

creation, act of. God's work of bringing into existence the natural and preternatural realms.

decretive will. God's sovereign will ordained as a firm decree that will happen without fail.

deism. Philosophy popular in the seventeenth and eighteenth centuries that teaches that after God created the universe, he left it to function on its own.

divine attributes. The perfections of God's essence revealed through a variety of historical manifestations.

divine immanence. Attribute of God referring to his closeness to man and creation; God's active involvement in space and time.

divine mysteries. Innumerable undisclosed truths about God that limit our understanding of God.

divine revelation. God's self-disclosure, always given in human terms and most fully given in Christ.

divine transcendence. Attribute of God indicating that he is superior to man and above all the limitations of the created universe, including space and time.

divine works. What God has done, what he is doing, and what he will do in the history of the world.

dualism. Theory that reduces a subject to the mutual existence of two opposing principles or entities.

economic. Term meaning "relating to household management"; used when speaking of how the three persons of the Trinity relate to one another.

Enlightenment, the. A philosophical movement of the seventeenth and eighteenth centuries that emphasized human reason over religious, social, and political traditions.

essence of God. The unchanging reality that underlies all of God's outward, changing manifestations.

essentia. Latin term meaning "essence" or "being."

eternal. Not restricted by time; without beginning or end.

eternal procession. Theological term used in reference to the Holy Spirit's relationship to the Father and Son."

eudokia. Greek term for "good pleasure," "favor."

ex nihilo. Latin term meaning "out of nothing."

fatalism. A view of the future that simply accepts what is to come because the events are inevitable; in this view, God is impersonal and does not interact with man.

First Cause. Theological term for God as the Creator and ultimate cause behind everything that happens in history.

foreknowledge. God's knowledge, prior to creation, of events that would occur in the course of history.

general revelation. God's use of the natural world and its workings to make his existence, nature, presence, actions, and will known to all humanity.

hagios. Greek word for "holy" or "set apart."

ḥāpēṣ. Hebrew term meaning "pleasing."

ḥāšab. Hebrew term meaning "to think," "to plan," "to determine."

Hellenistic. Of or relating to Greek civilization, culture, or language, after the time of Alexander the Great.

historical manifestations. The ways God involved himself with the unfolding of biblical history.

Hodge, Charles (1797–1878). Well-known theologian from Princeton Theological Seminary who wrote numerous commentaries, articles, and books, including his three-volume *Systematic Theology*.

image and likeness of God. Term used in theology to express the fact that man is made to be similar to God, but not equal, and is God's representative on earth.

immensity of God. Theological term referring to God's infinite, eternal, and unchangeable existence beyond creation.

immensus. Latin term meaning "immeasurable," "incalculable."

incommunicable attributes. Characteristics of God that cannot be communicated to man (e.g., omnipotence, omniscience, omnipresence, eternality).

incomprehensibility of God. Term used in theology to express the fact that we can know some things about God as he reveals them to us, but we will never know everything about God.

infinite. Immeasurable, incalculable, unending, unlimited.

infinitus. Latin term meaning "unlimited," "unending."

infra. Latin term meaning "beneath."

infralapsarianism. The belief that God's decree to save his people should be placed after his decree to permit the fall of humanity into sin.

lapsus. Latin term meaning "the fall."

mysticism. Belief system that emphasizes the need to go beyond reason to receive revelation through transcendent spiritual enlightenment.

natural theology. Humanity's ongoing attempt to learn about God through general revelation.

omnipotence. Almighty and unlimited power.

omnipresence. Existence in all places.

omniscience. Knowledge of all things.

ontological. Term meaning "related to being"; used to refer to the fact that all three persons of the Trinity possess the same divine attributes and essence.

open theism. Theological outlook that says the success of God's plans, purposes, and will are entirely dependent on history, especially on the choices that spirits and human beingsmake.

pantheism. Belief that identifies God with his creation.

patristic theology. Theology from approximately AD 150–600 that described, explained, and defended Christianity in ways that were relevant for Hellenistic cultures.

permanent divine mysteries. Truths about God that are beyond human comprehension.

pistis. Greek term for "belief," "faithfulness," "lovingkindness."

Plato (ca. 427–347 BC). Ancient Greek philosopher who studied under Socrates and founded the Academy at Athens.

polytheism. Belief in multiple gods.

prescriptive will. God's prescribed commands; his preferred will for humanity as revealed in his law.

preternatural. Describing the realm of existence that is beyond or beside nature; includes invisible spirits such as angels and demons.

prothesis. Greek term for "purpose," "plan."

providence. God's active involvement in history as he works out his eternal plan for creation and the welfare of his people.

providentia. Latin term with connotations of "attending to" or "taking care of" something.

qādôš. Hebrew term meaning "holy," "sanctified," "sacred."

rāsôn. Hebrew term meaning "pleasing," "favorable."

šāmayim. Hebrew term for "heaven," "the heavens," or "sky."

Scholasticism. School of philosophy taught by the academics (or "Scholastics") during the medieval period that put great emphasis on the use of Aristotelian logic and attempted to harmonize Christian theology with classical philosophy.

second causes. Created beings or objects that perform real but secondary roles in causing events to occur.

Septuagint. Greek translation of the Old Testament.

simple; simplicity of God. Theological term used to explain that God's essence is not a composite of different substances but a unified whole consisting of only one substance.

sovereignty. Theological term that refers to God's continuing rule and complete authority over all creation.

special revelation. God's disclosures of himself and his will to a select number of people through dreams, visions, prophets, the Scriptures, and other similar means.

sub. Latin term meaning "under."

sublapsarianism. Belief that God's decree to save his people came after his decree to permit the fall of humanity into sin, and that his decree to save came after his decree to offer redemption.

substantia. Latin term meaning "substance" or "essence"; used by Tertullian to refer to the oneness of God's being.

supra. Latin term meaning "above."

supralapsarianism. Belief that God's decree to save his people came before his decree to permit the fall of humanity into sin.

syncretism. The practice of mixing different religions or mixing philosophy with religion.

temporary divine mysteries. Truths about God that are hidden from human beings for a period of time and are revealed at some later point in history.

thelēma. Greek term for "will," "desire."

theological proposition. An indicative sentence that asserts as directly as possible at least one factual theological claim.

theological technical terms. Words and phrases with specialized meanings in theology.

theophany. A visible appearance of God to a human being or beings.

Trinity. Theological term used to express the fact that God is one essence in three persons.

via causalitatis. Latin phrase for "way of causation," referring to a way of learning about God by observing the good things he has created; part of the threefold strategy developed by medieval Scholastic theologians for pursuing natural theology.

via eminentiae. Latin phrase for "the way of eminence," referring to a way of learning about God by noting how God is greater than his creation; part of the threefold strategy developed by medieval Scholastic theologians for pursuing natural theology.

via negationis. Latin phrase for "the way of negation," referring to a way of learning about God by contrasting him with his creation; part of the threefold strategy developed by medieval Scholastic theologians for pursuing natural theology.

Westminster Confession of Faith. An ecumenical doctrinal summary composed by the Westminster Assembly of Divines and published in 1647.

Westminster Shorter Catechism. A traditional Protestant summary of Christian teaching; originally published in 1647.

yāʿaṣ. Hebrew term meaning "to give counsel," "to decree."

zamam. Hebrew term meaning "to purpose," "to plan."

BIBLIOGRAPHY

Aquinas, Thomas. *The Summa Contra Gentiles*.

Augustine. *On the Trinity*. Edited by Philip Schaff. Peabody, MA: Hendrickson Publishers, 1995.

Basinger, David, and Randall Basinger, eds. *Predestination and Free Will: Four Views of Divine Sovereignty and Human Freedom*. Downers Grove, IL: InterVarsity Press, 1986.

Bavinck, Herman. *The Doctrine of God*. Translated by William Hendriksen. London: Banner of Truth, 1978.

———. *Reformed Dogmatics*. Edited by John Bolt. Translated by John Vriend. 4 vols. Grand Rapids: Baker Academic, 2003–8.

Beisner, E. Calvin. *God in Three Persons*. Wheaton, IL: Tyndale, 1984.

Berkhof, Louis. *Systematic Theology*. New ed. Grand Rapids: Eerdmans, 1996.

Berkouwer, G. C. *The Providence of God*. Translated by Lewis B. Smedes. Studies in Dogmatics. Grand Rapids: Eerdmans, 1952.

Blocher, Henri. *In the Beginning: The Opening Chapters of Genesis*. Translated by David G. Preston. Downers Grove, IL: InterVarsity Press, 1984.

Bloesch, Donald G. *The Battle for the Trinity: The Debate over Inclusive God Language*. Ann Arbor, MI: Servant Publications, 1985.

Boettner, Loraine. *The Reformed Doctrine of Predestination.* Grand Rapids: Eerdmans, 1957.

Bray, Gerald. *The Doctrine of God.* Downers Grove, IL: InterVarsity Press, 1993.

Carson, D. A. *Divine Sovereignty and Human Responsibility: Biblical Perspectives in Tension.* Grand Rapids: Zondervan, 1994.

Charnock, Stephen. *The Existence and Attributes of God.* Reprint, Grand Rapids: Baker Books, 2000.

Craig, William Lane. *The Only Wise God: The Compatibility of Divine Foreknowledge and Human Freedom.* Grand Rapids: Baker Book House, 1987.

Erickson, Millard J. *Christian Theology.* Grand Rapids: Baker Book House, 1983.

Flavel, John. *The Mystery of Providence.* 1677. Reprint, London: Banner of Truth, 1963.

Frame, John M. *The Doctrine of God.* Phillipsburg, NJ: P&R Publishing, 2002.

———. *The Doctrine of the Knowledge of God.* Phillipsburg, NJ: Presbyterian and Reformed, 1987.

Gilkey, Langdon. *Maker of Heaven and Earth: A Study of the Christian Doctrine of Creation.* Garden City, NY: Doubleday, 1959.

Grudem, Wayne. *Systematic Theology: An Introduction to Biblical Doctrine.* Grand Rapids: Zondervan, 1994.

Harris, Murray J. *Jesus as God.* Grand Rapids: Baker Book House, 1992.

Haykin, Michael. "Defending the Holy Spirit's Deity: Basil of Caesarea, Gregory of Nyssa, and the Pneumatomachian Controversy of the 4th Century." *Southern Baptist Journal of Theology* 7, no. 3 (Fall 2003): 74–79.

Helm, Paul. *Eternal God: A Study of God without Time.* Oxford: Clarendon, 1988.

———. *The Providence of God.* Downers Grove, IL: InterVarsity Press, 1994.

Hodge, Charles. *Systematic Theology.* Reprint, Grand Rapids: Christian Classics Ethereal Library, 2005.

Kaiser, Christopher B. *The Doctrine of God*. Westchester, IL: Good News, 1982.

Kline, Meredith G. *Images of the Spirit*. Grand Rapids: Baker Book House, 1980.

———. *The Structure of Biblical Authority*. Grand Rapids: Eerdmans, 1972.

Kuyper, Abraham. *Principles of Biblical Authority*. Translated by J. H. de Vries. Grand Rapids: Eerdmans, 1968.

Lewis, C. S. *The Four Loves*. London: Geoffrey Bles, 1960.

———. *A Grief Observed*. 1961. Reprint, New York: HarperOne, 2001.

———. *The Problem of Pain*. 1940. Reprint, New York: HarperOne, 2001.

Macleod, Donald. *Behold Your God*. 2nd ed. Fearn, UK: Christian Focus, 1995.

McDonald, H. D. *Theories of Revelation: An Historical Study, 1860–1960*. Grand Rapids: Baker Book House, 1979.

McGrath, Alister E. *Understanding the Trinity*. Grand Rapids: Zondervan, 1988.

McNeill, John T., ed. *Calvin: Institutes of the Christian Religion*. Translated by Ford Lewis Battles. Philadelphia: Westminster Press, 1960.

Mikolaski, S. J. "The Triune God." In *Fundamentals of the Faith*, edited by C. F. H. Henry, 59–76. Grand Rapids: Zondervan, 1969.

Murray, John. "Calvin's Doctrine of Creation." *Westminster Theological Journal* 17.1 (November 1954): 21–42.

Packer, J. I. *Knowing God*. London: Hodder and Stoughton, 1973.

Palmer, Edwin. *The Holy Spirit: His Person and Ministry*. 2nd ed. Phillipsburg, NJ: P&R Publishing, 2005.

Percival, Henry R., ed. *The Seven Ecumenical Councils*. Series 2, vol. 14 of *A Select Library of Nicene and Post-Nicene Fathers of the Christian Church*. 1900. Reprint, Grand Rapids: Christian Classics Ethereal Library, 2005.

Pink, Arthur W. *The Sovereignty of God*. Grand Rapids: Baker Books, 1930.

Poythress, Vern S. *Knowing and the Trinity: How Perspectives in Human*

Knowledge Imitate the Trinity. Phillipsburg, NJ: P&R Publishing, 2018.

Reymond, Robert L. *Jesus, Divine Messiah: The New Testament Witness*. Phillipsburg, NJ: Presbyterian and Reformed, 1990.

———. *A New Systematic Theology of the Christian Faith*. Nashville: Thomas Nelson, 1998.

Schaff, Philip, ed. *The Creeds of Christendom, with a History and Critical Notes*. Vol. 1, *The History of Creeds*. 1877. Reprint, New York: Harper & Brothers, 1919.

Tozer, A. W. *The Knowledge of the Holy*. New York: Harper and Row, 1961.

Urban, Linwood, and Douglas N. Walton, eds. *The Power of God*. New York: Oxford University Press, 1978.

Vos, Geerhardus. *Biblical Theology: Old and New Testaments*. Grand Rapids: Eerdmans, 1948.

Warfield, Benjamin B. "The Biblical Doctrine of the Trinity." In *Biblical Doctrines*. Vol. 2 of *The Works of Benjamin B. Warfield*. Grand Rapids: Baker Book House, 2003.

———. *The Lord of Glory*. New York: American Tract Society, 1907. Reprint, Grand Rapids: Baker Book House, 1975.

———. "The Spirit of God in the Old Testament." In *Biblical and Theological Studies*, edited by Samuel G. Craig, 127–56. 1950. Reprint, Philadelphia: Presbyterian and Reformed, 1952.

Wenham, John W. *The Goodness of God*. London: InterVarsity Press, 1974.

Young, Davis A. *Creation and the Flood*. Grand Rapids: Baker Book House, 1977.

CONTRIBUTORS

The following contributors were interviewed on video by the staff of Third Millennium Ministries, answering a variety of questions related to the content of this volume. Transcriptions of their answers appear in the gray boxes throughout the text.

Andrew Abernethy is associate professor of Old Testament at Wheaton College and Wheaton College Graduate School.

Danny Akin is president of Southeastern Baptist Theological Seminary.

Vincent Bacote is associate professor of theology and director of the Center for Applied Christian Ethics at Wheaton College and Wheaton College Graduate School.

Voddie Baucham Jr. is dean of theology at African Christian University in Zambia.

Bruce Baugus is associate professor of philosophy and theology at Reformed Theological Seminary.

Sukhwant S. Bhatia is principal and professor of biblical studies and pastoral theology at North India Institute of Theological Studies in Chandigarh, India, and president and CEO of Seek Partners International, Inc.

Rick Boyd is associate professor of biblical interpretation at Wesley Biblical Seminary.

Gary M. Burge is dean of the faculty and visiting professor of New Testament at Calvin Seminary, having served previously as professor of New Testament at Wheaton College and Wheaton College Graduate School.

D. A. Carson is research professor emeritus of New Testament at Trinity Evangelical Divinity School and cofounder of The Gospel Coalition.

Matt Carter is lead pastor of Sagemont Church in Houston, Texas, having served previously as pastor of preaching and vision at The Austin Stone Community Church in Austin, Texas.

Gareth Cockerill is professor emeritus of New Testament and biblical theology at Wesley Biblical Seminary.

Larry Cockrell is senior pastor of Household of Faith Church in Birmingham, Alabama, and faculty member of Birmingham Theological Seminary.

Brandon D. Crowe is professor of New Testament at Westminster Theological Seminary and book review editor for the *Westminster Theological Journal.*

J. Ligon Duncan III is chancellor, CEO, and John E. Richards Professor of Systematic and Historical Theology at Reformed Theological Seminary.

William Edgar is professor of apologetics at Westminster Theological Seminary.

Bruce L. Fields (1951–2020) was chair of the biblical and systematic theology department and associate professor of biblical and systematic theology at Trinity Evangelical Divinity School.

Tim Foster is vice principal at Ridley College in Melbourne, Australia.

Matt Friedeman is professor of evangelism and discipleship at Wesley Biblical Seminary.

Michael J. Glodo is associate professor of pastoral theology at Reformed Theological Seminary in Orlando, Florida.

Dan Hendley is senior pastor of North Park Church in Wexford, Pennsylvania.

J. Scott Horrell is professor of theological studies at Dallas Theological Seminary.

Clete Hux is director and counter-cult apologist at Apologetics Resource Center in Birmingham, Alabama.

Keith Johnson serves as the national director of theological education for Cru (formerly Campus Crusade for Christ) and is a guest professor of systematic theology at Reformed Theological Seminary.

Craig S. Keener is the F. M. and Ada Thompson Chair of Biblical Studies at Asbury Theological Seminary.

Glenn R. Kreider is professor of theological studies at Dallas Theological Seminary.

Samuel Lamerson is president and professor of New Testament at Knox Theological Seminary.

Richard Lints is professor of theology and vice president for academic affairs at Gordon-Conwell Theological Seminary.

Bruce Little is director of the Francis A. Schaeffer Collection and emeritus professor of philosophy at Southeastern Baptist Theological Seminary.

R. Todd Mangum is professor of theology and academic dean at Biblical Theological Seminary.

Scott Manor is professor of historical theology and president of Knox Theological Seminary.

Josh Moody is senior pastor at College Church in Wheaton, Illinois.

Jeffery Moore served at Trinity Downtown Orlando as senior pastor from 2003 to 2014.

Grant R. Osborne (1942–2018) was professor of New Testament at Trinity Evangelical Divinity School.

Richard Phillips is senior minister of Second Presbyterian Church in Greenville, South Carolina, and chairman of the Philadelphia Conference on Reformed Theology.

Vermon Pierre is lead pastor for preaching and mission at Roosevelt Community Church in Phoenix, Arizona.

Paul R. Raabe is professor emeritus of exegetical theology at Concordia Seminary.

Harry L. Reeder III is senior pastor at Briarwood Presbyterian Church in Birmingham, Alabama.

Brandon P. Robbins is director of distance education at Birmingham Theological Seminary.

Ric Rodeheaver is senior pastor of Christ Community Church in Laguna Hills, California, and adjunct professor of practical theology at Christ Bible Seminary in Nagoya, Japan.

Steven C. Roy is associate professor of pastoral theology at Trinity Evangelical Divinity School.

Philip Ryken is president of Wheaton College.

Tim Sansbury is assistant professor of philosophy and theology and vice president of administration at Knox Theological Seminary.

Justyn Terry is academic dean of Wycliffe Hall, Oxford University, and was previously dean and president of Trinity School for Ministry in Ambridge, Pennsylvania.

K. Erik Thoennes is chair of theology and professor of biblical and theological studies at Biola University's Talbot School of Theology.

Stephen Tong is a Chinese evangelist and theologian, a promoter of the Reformed Evangelistic Movement, and the founder of the Stephen Tong Evangelistic Ministries International (STEMI) and Reformed Evangelical Church and Seminary in Indonesia.

Daniel Treier is the Blanchard Professor of Theology at Wheaton College and Wheaton College Graduate School.

Carl R. Trueman is professor of biblical and religious studies at Grove City College in Grove City, Pennsylvania.

Daniel B. Wallace is professor of New Testament studies at Dallas Theological Seminary.

Guy Waters is the James M. Baird Jr. Professor of New Testament and academic dean at Reformed Theological Seminary.

Sanders L. Willson served as senior minister at Second Presbyterian Church in Memphis, Tennessee, until retiring in 2017 and has served on the boards of The Gospel Coalition, Union University, and Reformed Theological Seminary.

Lewis Winkler is resident faculty member of theological and historical studies at East Asia School of Theology in Singapore.

INDEX OF SCRIPTURE

INDEX OF SUBJECTS
AND NAMES

Richard L. Pratt Jr. is cofounder and president of Third Millennium Ministries. He served as professor of Old Testament at Reformed Theological Seminary for more than twenty years and was chair of the Old Testament department. An ordained minister, Dr. Pratt travels extensively to evangelize and teach. He studied at Westminster Theological Seminary, received his MDiv from Union Theological Seminary, and earned his ThD in Old Testament studies from Harvard University. Dr. Pratt is the general editor of the *NIV Spirit of the Reformation Study Bible* and a translator for the New Living Translation. He has also authored numerous articles and books, including *Pray with Your Eyes Open, Every Thought Captive, Designed for Dignity, He Gave Us Stories, Commentary on 1 & 2 Chronicles*, and *Commentary on 1 & 2 Corinthians*.

Did you enjoy this book?
Consider writing a review online.
The author and editors appreciate your feedback!

Or write to P&R at editorial@prpbooks.com
with your comments. We'd love to hear from you.